This must-have book helps parents navigate parenting in a vastly different world from their own upbringing. We're providing it to all our clinicians to support patients in breaking generational trauma cycles and bring peace back to their households with its profound insights.

—**Liesl Perez, cofounder of Axis Integrated Mental Health, mother of four**

The Parent-Teen Connection is an insightful and transformative guide for parents navigating the often-tumultuous teenage years. A must-read for any parent seeking to create a nurturing and supportive environment for their teenagers.

—**Mary Gitau, MA, MSuic, founder and director of the Centre for Suicide Research and Intervention–Kenya, mother of two**

Susan's book provides a clear blueprint for navigating many difficult challenges. This is a single resource for struggling parents filled with real stories that resonate from our kitchen tables and living rooms. A must-have for parenting in today's wilderness!

—**Nelson Trujillo, MD, Boulder Community Health, father of three**

Susan's words are inspiring and deeply resonant, and her book is a valuable resource for parents, educators, and anyone working with young people. I highly recommend this book to anyone looking to make a positive difference in the lives of children and teenagers.

—**Jenna Clinchard, executive director, Rise against Suicide, mother of two**

The Parent-Teen Connection empathetically and clearly discusses how to become a trusted adult and how to navigate the many stressors impacting young people. This book is a critically helpful resource for parents or caregivers hoping to improve their relationships with their teenagers.

—**Lena MQ Heilmann, PhD, suicide prevention expert and sibling suicide loss survivor**

Praise for *The Parent-Teen Connection*

Susan Caso addresses the complexities of the parent-child relationship, spanning from infant bonding to homework stress to suicidal ideations. This is a handbook to help us all address the mental health epidemic that is affecting our young people.

—Shairi Turner, MD, MPH, chief health officer, Crisis Text Line, mother of two

The Parent-Teen Connection is an invaluable resource for any parent. Susan Caso takes readers on an immersive journey that allows you to develop insights into the cycle of interactions you have with your teen and how to purposefully shift your response to foster improved connectedness.

—Jessica Hawks, PhD, child and adolescent psychologist, clinical director, Pediatric Mental Health Institute, Children's Hospital Colorado, mother of two

Susan Caso has given families a precious gift: a roadmap for parents to understand and connect with their teens. This book is a must-read for any parent who wants to build an enduring, loving, and lasting relationship with their teenager.

—Tzivy Reiter, LCSW, director of Children's and National Trauma Services, Ohel, New York

The Parent-Teen Connection is an invaluable resource for parents aiming to create a secure, emotionally supportive environment for their teens. This book is a must-read for parents seeking to bridge generational gaps and cultivate a nurturing, emotionally close environment with their teens.

—Dr. Sally Spencer-Thomas, president of United Suicide Survivors International, mother of two

Susan Caso adeptly counsels readers on establishing trust and nurturing emotional bonds with their teens, imparting the skills necessary to cultivate an environment of open communication, validation, and unwavering familial support.

—Honey Beuf, executive director of The Liv Project, mother of three

Susan Caso has written a resource that we have long needed. Susan's warmth, combined with evidence-based practice and practical advice, makes this a welcomed and necessary resource.

—Matt Mishkind, PhD, deputy director of Johnson Depression Center, father of three

The

Parent-Teen Connection

How to Build Lifelong Family Relationships

Susan Caso, MA, LPC

Radius Book Group

New York

Radius Book Group
A division of Diversion Publishing Corp.
www.radiusbookgroup.com

Radius Book Group and colophon are registered trademarks of Diversion Publishing Corp.

For more information, email info@radiusbookgroup.com

The publisher does not have any control over and does not assume any responsibility for author or third-party websites or their content.

First Radius Book Group Edition: October 2024
Hardcover ISBN: 978-1-63576-936-4
e-ISBN: 978-1-63576-930-2

Book design by Scribe Inc.
Cover design by Jen Huppert
Interior graphics by Sorina Rosoiu

Printed in the United States of America
10 9 8 7 6 5 4 3 2 1

A Stand of Aspens: A Metaphor for Connectedness

Aspens are linked to each other by their deeply connected root system, creating a single organism, a family. They rely on each other and act as one collaborating system, working in unison. They are sensitive and respond to each other's needs in the grove, which brings resilience and their ability to thrive. Their collective strength is foundational. Aspens are grounded in belonging, yet each stands as a unique individual. It is known that a family of aspens produces a peaceful and comforting sound as their heart-shaped leaves rustle in the wind.

Contents

Introduction

Why I Wrote This Book

I heard a concerned mother's voice wavering on the phone. She conveyed a familiar, subtly alarmed tone, one I've used myself when worried about my own children. Sally had called to talk about her daughter Ella. Sally recognized something was "off" but didn't know what exactly. Ella seemed down and closed off and had been isolating in her room. She wasn't eating much at meals. She had stopped hanging out with friends after school and was spending more time gazing at her phone's screen, endlessly scrolling for updates. Sally and her husband tried to discuss it with her, and while Ella wouldn't share anything with them, she asked if she could see a therapist.

I met Ella a few days later. In our first session, Ella shared that each day felt like a struggle. She talked about the pressures she was facing at school and the difficulty she was experiencing navigating her social world. She felt alone in dealing with the reality of her life. Carrying it all by herself felt heavy, and there was a feeling of hopelessness. She shared that she wished things were different at home.

I asked, "What would 'different' look like?"

Ella said, "I want to feel comfortable talking to my parents about what is going on with me. Well, really, my mom. I want to be able to talk to her about how I am feeling. We just don't do that. It kinda feels like it's all business at home. We talk about school and what I need to get done, but we don't talk about how I am really doing. I guess it would be nice if I could feel emotionally close to my mother."

Ella wasn't the first teen I've heard say this. Many teens who come to my office tell me, "We don't talk about how we feel at home. I would like to feel closer to both of my parents."

The primary attachment between child and parent is the most critical. It feels natural for a teen to want to reach out to their parents for all sorts of questions and support in times of distress. Yet if we do not prepare the groundwork of open communication, which includes talking about feelings, communication attempts can bring hesitation and fear. That means teens begin sitting in tough feelings alone, which can be hard, confusing, and sometimes scary. Teens are left holding all their emotions themselves.

I asked Ella if she wanted my help to share her desire to be closer emotionally with her mother. She said yes. Her willingness to ask for this help was courageous. It speaks to the strong desire teens have for emotionally close relationships with their parents.

I then asked her, "How do you envision my support? Do you want to tell her with my support during a session? Would you like me to start the conversation while in a session with your mother? Or do you want me to share this without you in the room?"

Ella wanted me to talk with her mother without her being present. When teens respond with, "Please share with me, not in the room," they usually don't see how it would be possible to talk about their feelings with their parents.

I always offer these scenarios to give clients control over sharing openly with their parents, letting it be on their terms. I am always sending the message that any opening in communication in our sessions is good to share with your parents.

The most important connection a teen has is with their parents. That's where long-lasting change and support can happen. I don't want to be their therapist for the rest of their lives, but parents continue to be parents for life, so I ask, "Wouldn't it be best if you could talk this way with your parents, too?"

Of course, I think, "This is great news!" A child saying they want to share more with their parents and be emotionally closer—what could be better? I was jumping for joy at the progress that we could make now. So I emailed Ella's mom and asked her to come in.

Mom sits down, and I tell her, "Your daughter has shared that she wants to be comfortable sharing her feelings with you. She wants to be more emotionally close to you."

I could see Mom taking in what I had to say, nodding, thinking. There was a pause for a few minutes, and she said, "Okay, can you hand me a piece of paper and a pen"? I did.

She then asked, "How do I do that?"

I felt for Ella's mother. We only know what we know—our experience. Ella's mother's experience was not one of emotional closeness with her parents growing up.

The Generational Divide: Getting Comfortable Sharing Feelings

Adolescence has always been a time when teens begin to see their parents as human. They begin to "de-idealize" them. Naturally, the loss of idealization causes some friction in communication as parents sense the shift. Beyond that traditional gap, however, I can see an even wider generational gap between teens and their parents today regarding communication.

We have evolved in what we know to be healthy relational interactions and what our kids are watching from an early age reflects. Channels like Disney depict common preteen and teen issues and often model "best practice" interactions between parent and child in resolving those issues. Life doesn't often go like that in the real world, but our kids get frustrated when what is happening on the screen doesn't match what is happening at home.

Teens have easy access to endless information, and online discussions about mental health and the widespread use of psychological lingo in our culture have made them more emotionally aware. They want to have conversations about feelings—but this can create a wedge in the parent-teen relationship for those parents who've grown accustomed to not sharing feelings. I became determined to help families bridge these gaps and give them the skills to communicate and connect with heart.

Listening for a Living versus Listening to Your Child

I listen for a living, and I absolutely love my job! I help individuals—especially teens—make sense of what they are feeling. I help them see how their emotions drive their thoughts and actions. I'm able to do this for two reasons. First, because teens allow me to, which is an amazing privilege. Second, because I provide a safe space. I'm not going to tell them they're wrong for how they're feeling. I don't carry judgment for what they feel. I am just listening.

My relationship with teens is somewhat one-sided. I use my own emotions to help guide my time with my clients. I express how I feel about them in an empathetic way, but that is where it stops. They don't need to care for my emotions while trying to figure out their own. I don't carry along a history of injuries from my relationship with them, making our interaction a complex dynamic of debate, blame, and defensiveness—as sometimes happens with parents.

I provide a safe and supportive space for a client to be open and honest. They muddle through their own feelings with someone more or less holding their hand. As a result, they feel seen, heard, and validated in their own experience.

As a parent, you have a more difficult job than a therapist in listening to and interacting with your teen. The story within your relationship with your teen can get in the way, as you undoubtedly have developed a pattern of interaction during stressful moments. As your child has their emotions, you have your own feelings to maneuver through. A therapist listening and empathizing does bring reassurance and comfort to clients. However, when you listen and reassure your teen, it brings them even more comfort. That's thanks to the unique and powerful parent-child attachment bond.

Connectedness sketch

Parents and Teens Can Learn Skills to Create Connectedness

For Ella's mom, I drew the original "connectedness" heart-shaped graphic—borne out of twenty years of clinical practice and my experience with hundreds of teens.

Since it resonated with Ella's mom, I went home that day determined to find an easier way for parents and anyone in a relationship to understand how to create a safe connection. I wanted to create something easily digestible—especially for busy parents who need different ways of absorbing information.

Not discounting the interpersonal work involved, I knew a visual (or set of them) could help get key points across quickly while simultaneously sharing the whole picture. It is much easier to make headway toward a better and safer relationship within the parent-child relationship than in any other type of relationship.

As I began sharing the infographics with clients and speaking about connectedness at nonprofit organizations, mental health clinics, and school districts, I continued to refine the content. I have used many iterations of the graphics with parents and have seen a difference in how they relate to their children.

After their parents use these tools, teens in my office say things like "Mom hugged me today," "My parents really listened and just didn't lecture me," or "They apologized to me." I might even hear "My parents are changing for me."

From parents, I hear "My kiddo listens and connects with me now," "We have many things to bond over now, so we fight much less often," or "I can't believe I have my teen back."

In the beginning, I wanted some tools that would complement therapy. As time passed, I began to see their value. I realized to reach more parents, the next step was to write a book that encompasses the concepts behind the graphics.

What You Can Expect in This Book

The Parent-Teen Connection is designed to help you cultivate the feeling of connectedness with your teen. Ella's story shares a teen's desire to be emotionally close to her mother. Her mother shared the same desire but was unsure how to relate better with her teen, which brought emotional closeness. Many parents and teens are looking for closer connections; this is just one story. It may be your story too.

I used the word *teen* throughout this book to be concise, but *teen* should be considered synonymous with *preteen* and *young adult*. Adolescence ranges from ages ten to nineteen. The young adult age range is from fifteen to twenty-four. Ideally, the earlier we practice these concepts, the better, but there's a lifetime of influence between parents and their offspring. The overall concepts in this book are universal. However, modifications may be required in certain circumstances for a neurodiverse individual. Additionally, the terms *mom* and *dad* are used throughout the book. However, families come in all shapes and sizes. A teen could have two moms or two dads. There are both single dads and single moms. Grandparents, aunts, or uncles may be the primary parents. Families are also not necessarily biologically related. The term *primary caregiver* applies whenever *mom* or *dad* is written. There are many stories in this book about families, teens, and parents. Each person's name and identity has been changed to protect their privacy. All the stories of my family are true.

This book will show how to build trust with teens and strengthen your "felt connection." While critical to our ability to thrive, this feeling is almost in danger of extinction today.

Chapter 1 provides an overview of the connectedness concept. As you will learn, connectedness is a felt sense that is associated with a secure attachment.

Chapter 2 details why belonging is critical to your teen's mental health. While parents often assume their children feel like they belong at home, the reality is that many teens feel like outsiders in every setting today. I'll show you how to approach this delicate topic purposefully.

Chapter 3 explores communication, looking at typical patterns and frustrations between parents and their teens. We look at what's going on beyond the words said.

Chapters 4 and 5 delve deep into self-reflection, looking through an attachment theory lens at your past and present. We'll examine various influences that affect your parenting and communication styles today.

Chapter 6 looks at what might be going on between you and your teen and provides a framework to break down your patterns of interaction.

Chapter 7 explores external influences on teens and parents. I talk about the heightened pressure teens face today and will explore the nuances of mental health considering the "always on," hyperconnected world—including news, media, and social media. I'll offer some suggestions for setting healthy boundaries in this area.

Chapter 8 looks at the parents' relationship—whether married or divorced—and how conflict can impact your teen in many ways, including a secure attachment.

Chapter 9 concludes the book by looking at vulnerability as a stepping-stone to emotional transparency as well as illustrating how transparency and connectedness relate.

I wish you all the best in cultivating a strong connection with your teen that lasts a lifetime.

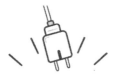

How to Create
An Environment that Fosters
Connectedness

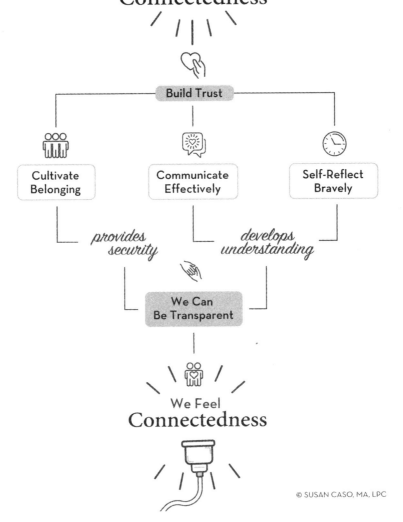

Build Trust

Cultivate Belonging

Communicate Effectively

Self-Reflect Bravely

provides security

develops understanding

We Can Be Transparent

We Feel
Connectedness

CHAPTER 1

Connectedness

Parenting. No Pressure, Right?

Every day as a parent is like the first day of a new job. Once you think you have it figured out, something changes. Your kid moves on to another stage of development, and you must pivot to meet their newest needs.

Connectedness

Kids have specific ways of being (their nature), but how you interact with them (your nurture) makes a significant impact on their development. Nurturing a child's development even impacts how certain biological aspects play out. Just as a seed holds potential for growth, that seed must be nurtured to bloom into a flower. Your teen needs daily nurturing through an emotional connection with you. How you "are" with your children impacts their well-being.

Parenting—from birth into adulthood—is an enormous role. Being your kid's mom or dad is just the beginning. You become their nurturer, safety monitor, moral compass, strategic planner, nutritionist, emotional nurse, confidant, taxi driver, chef, alarm clock, taskmaster, financial supporter, mentor, reality check, and cheerleader.

It can seem overwhelming, but the good news is you don't have to be a perfect parent. You don't have to be perfect in any of your relationships. The most essential thing in relationships is to *cultivate connectedness.*

The connection between a primary caregiver (usually a parent) and a child is typically the most critical connection the child will ever have. It's so much more than your child knowing you love them.

When adolescents talk about their relationship with their parents, they say, "I know they love me—they do a lot for me—but I am not sure how they really feel about

9

me." Parents do so much for their kids, and these actions do demonstrate love. However, often these labors of love are accompanied by stress and exasperation.

Often, I have parents do an exercise: write a letter to your child about how you feel about them and what you think of them. I read it in session to my clients. The response from my clients is essentially the same: "I had no idea they felt that way about me!" or "They see me that way?" I see such joy on their faces. It's one of the most powerful exercises.

People have many misconceptions about how others view them; kids question and make assumptions about how their parents think and feel about them. In close relationships, it is hard to believe these misconceptions go unverified because they impact each person involved and the relationship as a whole. Teens need to have approval and unconditional love from their parents. That approval isn't just about what they accomplish or produce but about who they are.

One Thing I've Learned in My Twenty Years as a Therapist

I have listened to the concerns of teens and young adults for more than two decades. Their relationships with their parents are a primary focus of our conversations. I may not have all the answers. What I do know is that we all thrive when feeling connectedness with one another. In twenty years of clinical practice observation, I've seen countless teens develop more open relationships with their parents, but it requires a conscious effort to foster connectedness.

Depending on what you read, there are somewhere between four and twenty-five parenting theories, and parenting advice has varied widely over the years. There was a time when parents used intimidation and kids feared their parents. Then Dr. Benjamin Spock, heavily influenced by Sigmund Freud's work, encouraged parents to move away from intimidation and instead shower kids with attention and affection. The approach was later criticized for being overly permissive. As a parent, you've no doubt witnessed how other "experts" have subsequently proposed parenting models that shape generational trends. We've all seen helicopter parents hover and heard of the snowplow or lawnmower parents who seek to remove all obstacles from their children.

Parenting: My First Day on the Job

I remember looking down at my firstborn in the middle of the night while she was crying on the changing table. I recall telling myself, "It is all up to me. This little person's life is in my hands. I can't mess this up."

From there, I thought, "Do I know how to raise this little person into adulthood? I have motherly instincts, but are they the right instincts? Do I know how to be a parent? Do I know what I am doing?"

First day on the job, and I didn't even know how to change a diaper! The panic of getting it right quickly set in.

Being a parent is the most important job you will ever have. No pressure, right?

And new pressures surface seemingly every day—well into adolescence.

So what's the approach to take that won't "mess up" your teen?

A parent-child relationship flourishes when it allows for openness and mutual respect, giving a feeling of being both understood and valued. This relationship feels safe and secure, so both parent and child can be more transparent and ultimately feel true connectedness.

This all might sound impossible. Your kids being "open and transparent" with you? Even as teenagers? Yes, it is possible.

The parent-child relationship is the most important connection. It can make all the difference in how teens view themselves. It's biological. And irrefutable. Your children look to you to tell them how they fit into this world. How you interact with them largely dictates how they feel about themselves.

The teenage years are when they learn how to relate to others in a relationship. They create the relationship dance that sets the tone for future relationships. They learn how to deal with life's stresses and challenges and how to ask for what they need and gain support from those close to them.

In a time when the world can feel particularly chaotic and unsafe, more than ever, kids need a safe landing place. That place needs to be in the parent-child relationship. That place is in your home, not just in their room by themselves.

Connections with family, peers, and community significantly impact human development. Researchers have found that connectedness with at least one parent helps teens "experience fewer emotional problems, fewer suicide attempts, less conduct disorders, better school performance, higher self-esteem, and less involvement in violence and substance use."[1] In addition, "youth who felt more connected to parents reported lower levels of depressive symptoms."[2]

Creating a Sense of Connectedness at Home

Connectedness directly impacts your mental health, physical well-being, and resilience in dealing with life stressors. It is a safety net, giving you someone to reach out to for comfort during difficult times. It provides you with a sense that you aren't alone.

How I Define Connectedness within Family

Connectedness is a feeling of emotional closeness with another who truly knows, accepts, cares for, and values us. There is warmth and responsiveness in the relationship that feels safe and reassuring. It positively impacts our self-worth and gives us the confidence to be open, explore, and grow by initiating new experiences.

While the modern world hyperconnects people in a certain sense—through digital platforms, text, videos, social apps, and so on—communication between two people has increasingly become asynchronous. When this happens, you lose the sense of shared emotion found when communicating in real life.

While we may feel more connected than ever due to technological advances, we are actually lonelier than ever. US Surgeon General Vivek Murthy's May 2023 report warned that the epidemic of loneliness and isolation stems from a lack of connection, noting, "Our epidemic of loneliness and isolation has been an underappreciated public health crisis that has harmed individual and societal health. Our relationships are a source of healing and well-being hiding in plain sight—one that can help us live healthier, more fulfilled, and more productive lives."[3]

Figuring out how to tackle this loneliness epidemic and the current state of adolescent mental health can feel overwhelming. Family influence is more than a solution—it is essential. Curing the loneliness epidemic begins with the parent-child connection.

The family unit is spending less and less time together due to families spreading out geographically, high divorce rates, rising costs of living that cause both parents to work more, an increase in technology use as a means to connect, and higher demands on youths' time in academics and extracurricular activities. With all the competing demands on time, families must proactively block out more time for one another. Family time may feel low on the priority list, but less time spent as a family unit means less frequent emotional connection. Every human needs this kind of genuine connection for physical and mental well-being. That includes your teen(s).

As shared in the introduction, the idea for the connectedness graphics originated as a precursor to this book to help families create stronger emotional bonds. Emotional closeness between parent and child is not just what is theoretically needed during this loneliness epidemic; it is what teens in therapy are asking from their parents. A cultural shift is needed, and it begins at home.

Building Trust in the Parent-Teen Relationship

Parents can cultivate a home environment with a strong sense of connectedness, and that starts with building trust. Any relationship requires trust before each person can feel safe and secure. Trust is a necessary anchor that secures any relationship.

Let's first look at what builds parent-infant trust. Psychologist and psychoanalyst John Bowlby studied the development of the early childhood years, specifically looking at the parent-child relationship through an attachment lens. He noticed that a parent's attunement and consistent attentiveness would create a secure bond. He noted that a lack of this would create insecure bonds.

Developmental psychologist Mary Ainsworth built on Bowlby's work, conducting experiments identifying four primary attachment styles—secure, anxious, avoidant, and disorganized.

Building Trust in the Parent-Teen Relationship

Several fundamental components foster this process of building trust, including creating a sense of belonging within your family and communicating effectively, which means sharing emotions, talking about feelings, and engaging in self-reflection to do that.

These elements—belonging, communicating, and self-reflection—provide security and understanding in the relationship. Once present, they allow us to be open and transparent with one another. When you are transparent in your relationships, you feel more emotionally close, creating a sense of connectedness.

Continually making it safe for your kids to be emotionally transparent with you builds trust. As teens constantly face new changes within themselves—cognitively, emotionally, and physically—they also face changes in their environment. When you are emotionally present to support, reassure, and comfort them, they can more openly communicate with you about their ongoing challenges.

Every day, teens are learning new material in their classes. They are trying to figure out how to live in their own rapidly changing bodies. Teens' social worlds present them daily with new situations to resolve. Now social media further complicates their lives.

Think of how you feel on the first day of a new job as an adult. You don't know much of anything. It's a new experience you are taking in and learning how to navigate. Change brings feelings of confusion, insecurity, and uncertainty. Yet in time, you will find your way. Your teen(s) will also flourish in time, so long as you parent mindfully and continually create psychological safety.

The Broken Christmas Ornament: Building Trust Early

One year at Christmas, I remember finding a broken ornament under the tree. I asked my youngest, who was five and standing nearby at the time, "Who broke this ornament?"

She said, "My sister."

Her sister was nineteen at the time. (I am laughing right now, thinking that she even thought to blame her sister, who was a decade and a half older . . . unlikely!)

I paused, took a deep breath, and said, "You won't get in trouble for breaking the ornament, but you will get a consequence for not telling the truth."

As expected, she came clean.

I always made it a point to let all my kids know that messing up wasn't going to get them in trouble. What could a five-year-old do that would really warrant severe consequences anyway?

Honestly, my main goals were to ensure my kids (1) could take responsibility for their mistakes instead of blaming external factors or other people and (2) could come to me whenever they messed up. Even if trust is broken, it can be repaired in a loving relationship.

Even if you build strong trust with your kids early on, the bad news is this: Your teen is going to break the trust you've built at some point. And it might hurt.

Where teens are in their brain development causes them to push boundaries, take risks, and try what is unthinkable to you. They are at a disadvantage. Their brains are telling them to venture out and try new things. Meanwhile, they haven't yet developed problem-solving capabilities and impulse regulation skills. A lack of skills is not an excuse for poor behavior—consequences will still exist for poor choices. Keeping developmental stages in mind may lessen the blow of them breaking your trust.

Trust between a parent and child is a relational necessity. The parent-child relationship is the first of many relationships kids will have—the first time they learn to trust another human. Parents need to ensure they are a trusting and reliable force in their kids' lives—even in the adolescent years. For a parent, it can feel like walking on a tightrope trying to balance positive connections while delivering demands.

We need to make sure we are not alienating our teens. A trusting relationship feels safe, accepting, and open. Building trust takes thoughtfulness, care, and self-reflection to maintain in the parent-child relationship, as it does in any other relationship.

One recent study looked at the link between teen anxiety and depression and the quality of the parent-teen connection. The connection included trust and communication with parents during the adolescent years (sixth grade to twelfth grade). Study coauthor Dr. Suniya Luthar reported, "Increases in alienation from both parents and decreasing trust between children and their mothers were related to higher levels of anxiety in grade 12. Depressive symptoms in grade 12 were also predicted by increasing alienation and decreasing trust with mothers during the high school years."[4]

The inability to trust causes uncertainty and instability. It evokes an uneasiness that you can't put your finger on. When trust is not present, a teen can't feel completely comfortable and will start to disconnect. Lack of confidence in another's reliability leads to distress, feeling unsafe, and questioning how the other person will react or respond.

You aren't free to be transparent about your feelings or be who you are at your core when trust doesn't exist. The same is true for how your teen feels. Uncertainty breaks the bond between a parent and teen, which prevents essential moments of secure bonding and building personal worth, competency, and interdependence.

When you think about it, children are in the most vulnerable position. They have little control over their lives and rely on their parents for emotional and physical care. Parents teach their teens whether it is safe to rely on someone else and to be emotionally close to others.

Dr. Sue Johnson's book *Attachment Theory in Practice* summarizes the parenting process like this: "We decide with caregivers what we can see and name, what will happen when we are lonely and afraid, whether it is best to voice or stifle our vulnerability, and how best to get a response from others. These scenarios are then written in our neurons and neural networks and become automatic; they are simply who we are!"[5]

Openness is necessary for close and meaningful relationships and a feeling of connectedness. Connectedness is a protective factor against anxiety, depression, and loneliness.

Building a sense of trust in your home and within your family unit is a necessity for closeness and your teen's well-being. There is no way around it.

Ideally, teenagers develop a strong trust that begets an internal monologue that sounds something like this:

"I trust my parents will . . .

- know how to parent me."
- take care of my physical needs."
- understand and care for my emotional needs."
- respond to me in an empathetic way."
- show me what a healthy relationship feels like."

"I trust that I . . .

- remain a priority in my parents' lives, even as I reach adulthood."
- can express how I am feeling such that my parents will listen to, comfort, and reassure me."

This is what teens need, and it's a parent's responsibility to provide a sense of trust that encompasses these ideals.

Attachment, Co-regulating, and the Parent-Child Volley

As a parent, you are your kid's primary attachment figure. Your parenting even has a biological effect on brain development. A child's experiences, both positive and negative, impact not only your child's academic growth but their emotional development. Emotional development includes how kids learn to feel, express, and regulate emotions. As Professor Karine Dubois-Comtois and colleagues shared in the *Journal of Child and Adolescent Behavior*, "Attachment becomes a state of mind which guides adolescents' behavior and thought, as well as stress regulation strategies."[6]

Philip A. Fisher, a senior fellow at Harvard University's Center on the Developing Child, describes parent-child interactions as "serve and return"[7]—like a tennis match, a child may "serve" up an emotion, such as distress or excitement, and if the parent responds in a warm and emotionally available way, that's a "return." This kind of "parent-child volley" occurs and evolves throughout childhood (zero to seven years).

For example, an infant's way of communicating any need to a parent is through crying. A little later, it becomes developmentally possible for them to communicate verbally. Parents use verbal exchanges as coaching moments, and the child uses them as observational learning of the expression of needs. If the environment is safe—if "serves" are regularly returned—a child can express their feelings and needs more clearly. Parents are then even better able to respond. However, if the parent misses a "serve," the child may feel unsafe to share. When the cycle breaks, the child's brain architecture changes accordingly.

Child-parent "serve and return" literally shapes neurocircuitry. Dr. Fisher's research has found that electrical signals in the brain form circuits that either strengthen over time through repeated use . . . or fade through pruning.

These kinds of reciprocal interactions have been shown to have huge positive effects on a child's development in the near term. In the long term, they affect a child's prosperity and well-being throughout the lifespan. Even something seemingly simple, such as basic cooing back and forth between caregivers and children, represents a volley that ultimately makes a big difference in a child's emotional state. The volley creates a willingness to share and bond with others throughout life.

"Serve and Return": Observing Parenting Volleys at Different Stages

Moments of "serve and return" between parent and child never go away. We need to volley with our teens as we did when they were infants.

Toddler	Teenager
Parent: [Reading a book] "The farmer said hello to the cow." Child: "Coo." Parent: "Is that the farmer?" Child: "Coo." [Points to a cow] Parent: [Makes eye contact, smiles, and uses an encouraging voice and inviting pitch that positively reinforces nonverbals] "Oh, that's the cow." Child: "Ga."	Parent: "What's going on in your world?" Teen: "Not much." Parent: "Not much, huh?" Teen: "Yeah." Parent: "Yeah." [Nods, pauses, establishes eye contact, observes] "You sound a little low." Teen: "Yeah." [Long pause] "I'm not sure if I want to go to the game." Parent: "Mm-hmm." [Listening nonreactively, staying present in the moment] Teen: "Well, I've been thinking about what to do . . ." Parent: [Verbalizing commitment to just listen, maintaining eye contact] "Okay, I'm here to listen."

A trust-building "serve and return" might be easier to accomplish during your child's early years. At that time, they are more transparent in needing something from you. They cry, and you tell yourself it must be one or more of three things: they need to eat, get a diaper changed, or be soothed by you holding them and rocking.

As your kids get older, the "serve" isn't as obvious. It looks different. You once again must use your intuition to assess their changing needs. It may seem they aren't serving the ball at all . . . or that they are rapidly and haphazardly flinging balls across the court to you.

A lot of baseline changes are going on for adolescents. They can feel awkward and unsure of themselves. They may tend to go inward and close off. They are navigating the social world and dealing with more pressures than ever. Insecurities can arise due to these changes. Teens are trying to figure out where they fit within their peer group—where they belong in life.

Too often, parents don't ask, don't listen, and don't recognize the "serve." They may compare a situation to a memory of their own teenage years, make assumptions, or otherwise minimize the teen's current experience.

Parents may seek to "problem-solve" rather than listen, or they may become instructional, give a lecture, or micromanage. They may not respect the teenager's growing autonomy and decision-making ability. These approaches obliterate trust.

When already overwhelmed teens find home life stressful or contentious, they may shut down or rise up in conflict. These reactions represent an effort to maintain their stability and to keep themselves safe. They can feel lost navigating it all. They may feel they can no longer reach out to their primary attachment figures (their parents) to sort it all out.

Additionally, natural defense systems may cause a "serve" to be returned by the parent in a way that causes conflict. A teen may feel like the parent has begun pelting them with a series of "return aces." In the long term, the kid stops serving.

As your kids grow and develop, you must continually build trust so they will come to you when they are struggling. You want them to remain transparent, serving up signals like when they cried out as infants. You want them to reach out to you with their psychological stress.

Building trust happens by creating a sense of belonging and paying attention to how you communicate. What you communicate about can create feelings of safety and understanding (or not). Every parent must continually self-reflect and then take all the steps needed to build trust.

Barriers to belonging are also injuries to the attachment between parent and child. Everyone has strategies to protect themselves from being hurt. When you've been hurt by others' rejection, judgment, and criticism, you feel you don't belong. Coping strategies may include withdrawing, rising up and defending, or doing anything possible to get positive or negative attention. When your teen becomes defensive, instead of defending yourself or delivering a consequence, be curious.

When you can create an environment where you feel safe and can be open, kids get into a pattern of serving up. You get into the habit of returning. Yes, it is a little more emotional work to return a teenager's mood swings, verbal jabs, and loaded glances without getting upset than to return a baby's coos and cries. However, once you know the game, "serve and return" becomes a continuous cycle that feels good to both parties.

Being your kid's primary attachment figure also means you have an incredible ability to comfort them. When they are infants, you comfort them mainly through co-regulating tasks. You soothed your infant with movement, sounds, and physical touch—such as rocking, humming, singing, and cuddling. You anticipated and read their cues and learned to take specific actions to comfort them. Parents' responsiveness regulates emotions by bringing security to their children. Over time, this cultivates a "secure attachment." Eventually, with enough serves and returns, the child feels, "My parents are consistently there for me. I will get what I need. I feel safe."

This idea of co-regulating that brings secure attachment (and the warm feeling of connectedness) can still happen into adolescence and adulthood; it just looks slightly different. With secure attachment during adolescence, the "serve-return" consistency is achieved through parents' sensitivity, attunement, and emotional closeness.[8]

Physical closeness—touch such as hugs, kisses, and cuddling on the couch—still exists. Yet as the teenage brain develops, parents' comfort and reassurance occur through emotional connection too. The "return" in adolescence requires parents to become more sensitive to what teens are experiencing emotionally. You must listen more carefully, understand more intuitively, and relate more thoughtfully to really "get" what your teen may be going through.

You can talk to your kids about their feelings, be there to listen, and spend time cultivating the relationship. These actions co-regulate, calming a teens central nervous system. This effort will bring emotional safety and foster stronger emotional connections.

Takeaway: Parenting Teens Presents Opportunities for Comfort and Growth

During adolescence, teens start spending more time with their peers and less time with their parents, but parents still are the major influence on their children. The parent-child attachment is imperative for their growth and mental well-being.

Conflict can increase during adolescence. Instead of viewing this conflict as rebellion, parents need to understand their teen is exerting independence, venturing out, and exploring. Parents who remain open and work to understand their teen show commitment to the relationship. It is an opportunity to teach and build trust.

Beyond co-regulating, the volley provides a way to handle conflict. This serve-and-return process allows both parent and teen to feel seen, heard, and validated. Volleying provides you the structure to proceed through difficult or sensitive parent-teen interactions.

Emotional connections bring feelings of security and comfort—the idea that someone will always be there for us as needed. Teens (and all adults, for that matter) grow more confident when they experience this feeling of connectedness behind secure attachment.

Teens become more likely to try new things and stand on their own when they know someone will always be beside them. Everyone wants to feel someone has their back—no matter what. No one wants to feel alone emotionally.

This leads us to the subject of chapter 2, belonging.

Chapter 1 Reflection: Parent-Teen Connection

- What do you imagine your teen's current experience is in their relationship with you?
- What experience do you want for your teen in their relationship with you?

CHAPTER 2

Belonging

A Biological Need to Cultivate Belonging

A human biological need for belonging is what drives you to connect with others. Teens try to connect to "find their people" among their peers, to find where they feel like they most belong. In teens' social climate today, this task is met with an abundance of rejection. It's not like the days when you were silently searching for your sense of belonging among your peers while at school, in sports, or in other extracurricular activities. Now it's a 24/7 mission. Social media is a constant indicator of whether teens belong or not. They continually face questions like "Will I be blocked, ghosted, or taken off someone's story?" "Am I included in the latest event?" "Am I going to be accepted?" or "Will I belong . . . today?"

You as a parent have minimal control over whether your kids find their people outside your home. But you can impact their sense of belonging at home. It is a safety net that is essential for their well-being.

Being part of a family doesn't automatically give a child the feeling of belonging. You have to cultivate it.

Thinking of where a person belongs, the image of "home" may come to mind. That seems logical, but it isn't always the case. For many, home can actually feel unsafe. Parents need to be conscious of how their kids feel and how they interact with their kids. Regardless of a parent's intentions, barriers to a teen's felt sense of belonging include judgmentalness, criticism, teasing, lack of attunement, and verbal and nonverbal aggression.

You may assume your kids naturally feel they belong at home as part of your family unit, but you can verify these assumptions. It is the teen's own experience of a situation that matters most to them, just as your experience matters most to you. It's possible to improve the way you signal to your teens "You belong here" by observing your interactions and asking them how they feel.

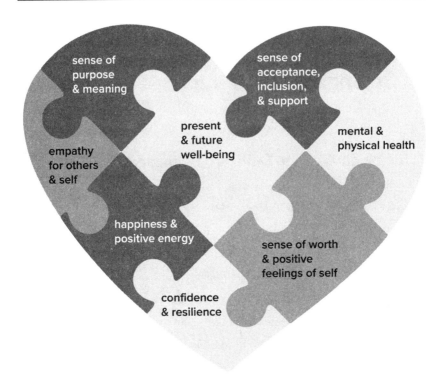

Benefits of belonging

You feel at home where you can breathe a sigh of relief, be yourself, and not worry about being accepted or rejected. You want a refuge from the chaotic world and respite from a difficult day. You want a place that feels full of warm and loving connections. Everyone craves such a place.

Teens especially need home to be a place where they feel they belong—where they feel safe from rejection. The need to belong at home applies regardless of race, ethnicity, culture, socioeconomic condition, gender identity, or religious orientation. It is one thing all humans have in common.

Creating a sense of belonging at home needs to be a continual, conscious task. According to a recent study in the *European Journal of Investigation in Health, Psychology and Education*, "People have a fundamental need for a psychological and emotional feeling to belong to someone and something that they hold dear."[1] The biological need to sense belonging to a primary caregiver too often goes unmet. No matter the biological relation of family members, everyone must actively work to foster belonging.

Defining a Sense of Belonging at Home

Belongingness brings a feeling of warmth and comfort. You feel you belong when you can let go of pretense and just be yourself. Teens likewise feel most accepted when they can be their true selves—exposing all parts of themselves, even the messy parts. They want to feel seen and heard. They want to feel included, respected, and valued. They may make mistakes, but they don't have to wonder if others approve of the person they are. There is no doubt that they "fit in." Belonging happens in predictable, familiar, and safe environments.

Teens want to feel connected, part of a bigger whole. They feel acceptance for who they are—and even for who they are not.

The family of origin is the first place children experience a relationship. Children learn many behaviors indirectly—from simple observations of their relationships with their parents. They take that experience into every relationship they have in the future. When they have a sense of belonging in their family of origin, they can better identify and create it in their relationships outside their home. Parents lead this ongoing task. It may not always seem like it, but children witness and mimic their parents' established (or absent) sense of belonging at home. Kids model what they see and enter their community equipped to find and develop a sense of belonging with peers—or not.

One study looking at the role of family belonging reported, "Adolescents' sense of family belonging is predictive of belonging to the peer and school context. . . . Previous studies . . . have acknowledged the importance of family relationships for children's capacity to develop strong and positive relationships with others outside the family."[2]

Secure attachment comes from a warm, loving, nurturing environment. Securely attached children have a deep sense of belonging, which leads to a feeling of connectedness.

As reported in the *Journal of Marriage and Family*, "An adolescent's perception of family belonging will be influenced by the quality of relationships that exist between family members. Although all family relationships have the potential to contribute to a child's sense of belonging, relationships with parents are likely to be key."[3]

Secure attachment typically develops between ages zero and seven years (infancy and early childhood). However, the need for a secure attachment between parent and child never goes away. It must be continually cultivated. The daily process of cultivating attachment in later years (eight to twenty-five years) builds on components learned in the early years, but there are distinct differences in this process. This makes sense given the challenges kids face as they grow. Parental support must also evolve during the emotional and cognitive maturing process.

In other social constructs, you can have a sense of belonging without secure attachment—there are nuances. Yet in the parent-child relationship, it's clear that you need belonging for secure attachment.

Why a Sense of Belonging Matters

"Belonging" is foundational. It's a biological need. Historically, people banished from their group or "tribe" could not survive. People will always need one another for companionship, to abate loneliness, for physical and mental well-being, and to care for one another. Humans are relational, and life is meant to be shared.[4]

Creating a sense of belonging is something parents often overlook but can learn to facilitate consciously. Additionally, a sense of belonging at home increases feelings of altruism, generates loyalty, and provides an atmosphere where the much-needed skill of empathy can be cultivated. Paying attention to whether our kids feel like they belong at home holds enormous benefits.

Given that parents represent the most significant influence in a child's life, it only makes sense that belonging to their family of origin would be the greatest need of belonging. Children long for a secure bond with their parents. Belonging means identifying with a group and feeling safe within that group. When teens identify with their family of origin and feel they belong, it strongly enhances their well-being.

Belongingness is a protective factor. It fosters resilience. Sensing that you aren't alone in navigating life's challenges brings security. Family remains the central influence in teens' lives—showing them whether and how they belong.

Ensuring Your Teens Feel They Belong at Home

Ensuring kids feel like they belong at home starts with *unconditional acceptance,* as indicated above. Your teen needs to know you value them for who they are at their core. They do best when they know your feelings for them do not depend on their choices. When they understand how you feel about them doesn't change because they make a mistake. Unconditional acceptance builds a child's self-worth. And isn't building self-worth a big part of parenting?

Showing your teen they have your unconditional acceptance matters because at some point, your teen *will* make a poor choice, mess up, and fall short of your expectations. Please remember they are learning, and their growth largely depends on trial and error. The fact is, they should mess up while in their parents' care. It allows parents to catch them, help them navigate, and ensure they still feel loved and accepted through it all. Providing unconditional acceptance through missteps allows teens to learn from their mistakes and gain better decision-making skills (problem-solving). Perhaps more importantly, they learn it is okay to make a mistake. A future mistake won't make them feel worthless or send them into a state of panic, worrying they have messed up. Acceptance brings self-compassion and kindness in the light of an error. It builds resilience.

Please keep in mind that unconditional acceptance doesn't mean failing to give natural consequences when teens' behavior warrants them. Parents still guide teens to achieve and reach their goals. Unconditional acceptance simply means that parents love their children at all times, and this feeling doesn't depend on a teen's ability to mold themselves into any specific expectation.

Your acceptance of them may not always seem more important than the acceptance of their peers, but it is. In a teen's mind, their parents know them best. You have known your children longer than anyone else and have seen their ups, downs, highs, lows, embarrassing moments, triumphs, and disappointments. Parents have the rare gift to show kids they are accepted entirely, including the parts they may not like about themselves.

Reviewing the Ways You Spend Time with Your Kids

Teens often say they feel a separateness in their house. When everyone gets home, they go to their private corners. Everyone is *so* busy with their own thing, including work for parents. No one comes out of their room. Teens also describe home as feeling like living with strangers under the same roof. When they don't share feelings, family members remain unaware of how any other family member is *really* doing. It can feel lonely and isolating. Everyone on their screens, living separate lives under the same roof, contributes to a growing disconnection within families today.[5]

Being a parent is hard! You are responsible for a lot. As your kids get older, life gets busy. As they gain more responsibilities, you can get stuck in the to-dos of life—both theirs and yours. You may find yourself tending to what needs to get done rather than to emotional needs.

One of our obligations as parents is to keep our teens on task, helping them with their to-do lists and making sure they are successful. If they aren't on track, you may think it reflects poorly on you and your parenting. Yet only connecting with your kids about logistics leaves little room for positive interactions and emotional connection.

Put yourself in your teen's shoes. After being told what to do at school all day, they don't want to hear any more directives. It's true for adults too. Spouses don't like it when significant others walk in the door and point out incomplete projects. It can feel more like a performance review than a relationship.

When teens estimate the percentage of interaction with their parents that they consider positive, most say it's around 30 percent. The negative 70 percent of parent-teen interaction reflects parents saying things like "Did you do this?" "Why didn't you complete that?" "You need to . . ."

How do you change the ratio of positive to negative interactions to build more positivity and a sense of belonging? One way is to become conscious of the time you spend in a "mom/dad" role versus the "parent" role.

The Mom/Dad Role versus the Parent Role

The mom/dad role is the warm, soft, humorous, loving, and fun side. This is when you are enjoying being with each other. Doing things like relaxing, listening to music, being silly, talking, playing games, preparing meals, and laughing together. Cultivating the relationship. This is when your teen feels your love the most. The mom/dad role is where true connection can happen. Trust is being built. Your kids know you love them, but with time spent in the mom/dad role, they feel you like them. They feel you want to spend time with them. This opens up the relationship for sharing, creating a safe landing place. Letting go of the to-do list and inviting true relaxation with you quickly allows home to be their sanctuary. Being comforted and reassured by you will come more easily when sharing both quality and quantity of time with you. The mom/dad role is time spent cultivating the most important part of the dyad, the relationship.

The parent role is the stuff you surely don't like doing, but it has to be done. This is making sure your teen is on track, doing their homework and chores. These are all the interactions that begin with, "Have you . . . ?" "You need to . . . ," or "When are you going to . . . ?" These often less pleasant interactions begin with rushing, repeated direction, and exasperation. You can imagine how these might not be relationship-building interactions. The parent role feels instructional. In these moments, you may personally want to run the other way. Your kids probably want to run too, as they either isolate themselves in their rooms or stop listening.

In a perfect world, you could be in the mom/dad role most of the time. When looking over the years, the mom and dad roles represent times when your kids relax, open up, and feel the most of your love. Those times build the foundations of close relationships.

The parent role, while necessary, can sometimes cause a teen to disconnect. When the relationship focuses only on what the child is producing or not producing, it can feel like you're only pointing out how they aren't measuring up. It feels negative.

Parents and kids each spend the day churning through tasks and producing outputs. So make your home feel like a refuge from the day. Aim for parent-teen interactions that they would consider at least 80 percent positive to 20 percent negative. When cultivating positive interactions, make sure you're doing something you both enjoy. It's not just about what the parent wants to do or wants their teen to do.

To accomplish this positive-to-negative ratio, cut down on daily nagging and reminders. Set aside specific times to discuss the less-than-fun things. For example,

- Check in about school-related tasks for fifteen minutes every couple of days, as noted on a calendar or planner.
- Before going to bed, have everyone take five minutes to pick up stuff in the common areas.
- Saturday mornings, blast music while everyone cleans their personal space and helps with the common areas. The motivation? Completing tasks so you can all move on to spending time together doing fun things or having friends over.

Share with your kids that you want to cut down on negative interactions to create more enjoyable time together. This helps them realize how much they mean to you. Your kids will appreciate that you are trying to better your relationship. More time spent in the mom/dad role undoubtedly results in less time in the parent role.

Ways to Spark Belonging

Sparking belonging means accepting their stage of development, creating traditions that matter to everyone, and consistently showing attention and affection.

Acceptance—Respect Teenage Executive Development

It is hard to feel a sense of belonging without feeling respected. Historically, teens have been labeled with words like *moody, rebellious, surly, difficult, delinquent, bad, dramatic,* and *problematic.* Often teens share that they don't feel respected by teachers, parents, and other adults.

Teens deal with developmental changes that drive how they function day to day. Their brains are still under construction. The prefrontal lobe—responsible for executive functioning—isn't fully developed until the midtwenties, with males (on average) maturing later than females. This part of the brain houses the abilities to problem-solve, regulate emotions, and reason.

In a time when our young teens are often expected to function at a college level both academically and with their extracurriculars, you can imagine how hard that might be when the part of their brain that houses organization and regulating emotions isn't fully developed.[6]

Yet teens are being asked to organize, stay on task, plan, juggle multiple tasks, problem-solve, and tolerate stress. That's like asking a young child to take over the carpool before they can even see over the dashboard, much less be of age to get a driving permit. They can't reach the pedals yet, which brings much frustration to both teens and parents.

When teens get overwhelmed by the tasks required of them, they need each parent to be a support, an ally, and a coach who meets them with understanding. Keep in mind that teens may seem more mature in certain areas of their lives than others. This is typical teenage development.

Understand Teens Naturally Individuate and Differentiate at This Age

Part of acceptance is respecting your child's natural process of development. Both individuating (exploring and creating a sense of self) and differentiating (creating a sense of self in the context of the family or distinct from family) are important pieces of a teen's development. These developmental tasks begin early in childhood yet seem most prominent during the adolescent years.

Differentiating and individuation are important stages in adolescence and a time when teens need your acceptance more than ever. Teens are figuring out who they are and where they fit in the world. They are making their own choices, voicing their opinions, and exploring their identity. Teens basically try on different hats to see which fits best. Parents understanding this as a normal positive developmental stage is important. It can feel so empowering to your teen when you accept them no matter what color their hair is and what style of clothes they are wearing. Judging, criticizing (verbally or nonverbally), or making fun of them for their style and choices can have lasting negative impressions on your child. It can interrupt the process of teens defining their sense of identity and what makes them unique. Parents are the lift-off pad to this lifelong process and can be an integral part of their teens' confidence in establishing their individuality.

Being open-minded, curious, and interested in their choices builds their confidence. They think, "I am able to try something new and still be accepted," "I can express myself in a different way and still feel I belong," or "I can voice my opinion, which may not be the same as that of my parents." As a bonus, when they feel your acceptance, they are more likely to be open with you. Your acceptance brings openness and closeness.

Parents may develop fears at this time. They have concerns when they see kids trying on new identities through their appearance and with their friend groups. They see their kids' opinions beginning to differ from their own. This can spark fear about what identity shifts mean for the long term, and it can also indicate a parent's own lack of comfort with the change, which makes it about you and not about them. A parent's self-reflection is important here.

Now that's not saying you don't need to set healthy boundaries. Teens need parents to establish "reasonable" boundaries. That actually shows you care. It also helps a teen feel safe knowing what is and is not acceptable.

It can be a hard balance to keep teens safe during this time while still allowing them to explore and discover. Teens require healthy boundaries that don't cross the line into criticism or shaming (see "Judgment and Criticism Push Teens Away" section below for examples of each).

During this important time of individuation, parents often feel some grief. They feel the shift of their child moving away from them and see them wanting to spend more time with their friends. They say "I miss my little one" and things like "They don't want to spend time with me. They don't need me anymore. Closeness seemed easier when they were little because they were my 'mini me' and wanted to hang with me all the time."

The grief sometimes translates into feelings of betrayal. Parents express feeling betrayed in some way that their teen doesn't want to spend as much time with them.

The relationship looks different. However, teens are just doing what they're supposed to be doing, individuating.

It's important for parents to know this is a healthy stage and not to take it personally that their teen doesn't want to hang out with them *as much*. They are naturally transitioning to more time spent in their social circles.

However, parents need to create a daily connection point to reinforce feelings of belonging with their teens. Just because they want to be with their friends more doesn't mean they don't need their parents. They still do!

Embrace Teens' Whole Identities: Evolving Gender Norms Matter

Teens now are teaching parents a lot about "belonging" related to expressing their sexuality and gender identification. They don't want to be put into the constructs that have been created over time around traditional gender roles. These are the "norms" of the past. They don't want to be identified by who they are attracted to, what they look like, or which gender they express. They do not want to hide who they are.

One study found that LGBTQ young adults who report high levels of parental rejection are eight times more likely to report attempting suicide and six times more likely to report high levels of depression.[7]

Jacob's Story: Layers of Stress Point to a Need for Acceptance

I met Jacob when he was twelve and his parents were going through a divorce. Although his parents were getting along, it was a hard adjustment for him. He was splitting his time between homes and struggling with seeing each parent less often.

Sessions started out with him talking about the stress of dealing with his parents' separation, but talk soon shifted to his feelings about his sexuality. He discussed feeling unsure of who he was attracted to and felt ashamed of the idea that he might be more attracted to males than females.

As sessions progressed, Jacob felt he was gay. He described an internal battle of whether to tell his parents, fearing their response. Sexuality was not something his parents ever discussed, and he was unsure of their beliefs.

Jacob felt he had to hide a huge part of himself, worrying they wouldn't accept him. He said, "What if I tell them, and they are angry with me? What if they won't look at me or treat me differently? Even worse, what if they don't want anything to do with me?" His distress was palpable.

We worked together for months around multiple subjects, dealing with the stress of adjusting to living in two different homes, losing family time with both parents present, and how to express the truth about his sexuality. After months of sharing space together, he felt he was ready to tell his parents, with support in session.

Rejection will happen to your teens outside of your home. Parents can give kids one place where they are free from rejection, where they don't have to hide any parts of themselves. Home needs to be the anchor in this sometimes cruel world.

Parents are responsible for raising their child to be a good human. One that is empathetic, compassionate, honest, trustworthy, and kind. A good human isn't dictated by how they dress, who they are attracted to, or what gender they express. If you aren't accepting, you might be alienating. It is painful for teens to feel alienated from the most important sense of security they need: the parent-child relationship.

Invite Collaboration to Build Decision-Making Skills for Adulthood

One universal parental goal is to keep teens safe from harm. This is a continual task as a parent that brings much anxiety. When your kids were young, keeping them safe was very labor intensive. The guard rails were up and close. As they mature, there is a need to widen the guard rails to allow them to flourish. Knowing when and where to put up guard rails for teens and when to pull them back as they reach adulthood becomes a challenging process. It may require you to continually monitor whether your teen is doing something that jeopardizes their physical and emotional safety.

Collaborate but Retain "Veto Power"

From the time my kids were young, I have looked at parenting as "collaboration with veto power." Collaboration is empowering, gives everyone a voice, and feels like pulling together to accomplish a goal. It's an exchange of knowledge that breeds learning for both. Hearing a teen out—while retaining veto capability—helps both parties stay open-minded.

I have learned so much from my own children. When I stop, listen, and approach with curiosity, things go much better. When I ask questions instead of telling them what to do, it generates thought on their part, and they gain problem-solving skills.

When you can collaborate with your teen on their path to adulthood, they feel respected. They have input in their own life and most likely give more thought to their decisions.

You know the feeling when a boss just dictates and micromanages you. You feel small. But when a boss asks your opinion and collaborates, you feel like your voice has value.

Obviously, no one wants to hear the negative *no*. To a teen, *no* translates into "You don't think I am mature enough," "You don't think I am capable," or "You don't trust me."

Your kids gain confidence when you give them opportunities to collaborate with you. When your teen feels that you listen and value their opinion, it elevates their view of self, and they are more likely to be responsible. Teens can help set basic rules and the consequences for breaking them, and decision-making that affects their day-to-day lives helps them feel empowered. Gaining buy-in while setting the rules helps ensure they follow the guidelines you set together. You will spend less time saying no. Collaboration gives teens the feeling of "We are in this together," creating a sense of belonging.

Traditions Cultivate a Sense of Belonging

Our entire society went through a trying time with the COVID-19 pandemic and lockdowns. Everyone was forced to cancel important occasions with loved ones. There was disappointment in not being able to follow established traditions. It was hard! It was an example of how meaningful even simple traditions are with family and close friends.

How do you incorporate traditions? When developed with intention, traditions can act like a glue that binds the family together. They can serve as a reminder that you belong to a specific group of people. Tradition can bring a sense of togetherness that feels warm and comforting. They give purpose and structure in coming together that also speak of family values and beliefs. Traditions can be around celebrations and recognition of successes. Such milestones allow one to be seen and valued by family members. They spread joy and nurture family connections and bonding. Traditions can create empathy and a sense of belonging if done well.

Cultural traditions give a teen a sense of community and shared identity. Passing down traditions from generation to generation gives meaning to our lives. Rituals and routines serve as connectors. Traditions create memories and encourage reminiscing. Such memories can bring security, comfort, and "good feels."

Recognize That Heartwarming Daily Habits Signal Belonging

Gathering for a meal can be hard today. Teens' schedules can be packed with academics, extracurricular activities, and time with friends. But finding time to gather as a family is important when cultivating a sense of belonging.

The Daily Recap: Interrogation or Intrigue?

During mealtime in our house, we have a tradition of sharing about our day. I have found that just asking "How was your day?" can land flat.

The response is usually a one-word answer: "Fine." That really tells you nothing.

Instead, we each share three things: the best, worst, and funniest things that happened to us that day. It may seem silly, but it sparks ideas and gives direction to the sharing, and we find out a lot! It makes mealtime last longer too.

We do have one rule ... your worst can't include anyone at the table.

Such rituals foster belonging and help teens get into the pattern of telling parents what's going on. Regular family conversations help kids see parents as approachable, even with the difficult stuff. A daily chat gives everyone the chance to listen, empathize, and gain an understanding of what everyone else is going through. Teens learn how to listen well, develop altruism, and engage in empathetic communication. Parents have an opportunity to comfort their teen, helping them feel less alone in whatever they may be struggling with that day, increasing the sense of family belonging.

Create Some New Traditions, Rituals, and Habits

Maybe you aren't getting the warm fuzzies from some of the current traditions that are in place. You and your teen can create new ones. Talking about traditions can be a fun conversation that allows both of you to brainstorm and collaborate.

You can have daily, weekly, and special occasion traditions that bring good feelings to you both. For example, try having breakfast together if dinner has become too challenging given the demands of after-school activities and homework. Hold a weekly karaoke or charades night. Listen to live music or try cooking or cultural activities once a week. Establish board game night. Celebrate the end of each school term with their favorite activity. Remember to focus on the conversation and connection, not performance. Teens still like to be silly and have fun.

Share Your Extended Family Stories

You likely have heard the saying, "It takes a village to raise a child." Parents lean on the support of their family and nearby networks, but the villages are shrinking. Over recent years, extended families increasingly live in different areas of the country.[8] Grandparents, aunts, uncles, and cousins have spread out geographically, leaving less of a village.

While parents have fewer family members to rely on for help, kids have less contact with their extended families. As a result, they hear fewer family stories. You may grumble when Grandpa tells a story *again and again*, but when kids hear such tales, they gain a valuable component of the sense of belonging.

Cultural and traditional exposure reinforces the feeling of belonging. Close access to extended family translates into support and stability, and research shows this increases self-esteem.[9] Kids also get the sense that more of their loved ones are there for them.

Extended family can also be stressful at times, especially when there are specific expectations or complicated past events. However, spending time with a supportive extended family can enhance your child's sense of belonging. It can be grounding to spend time with people who've known one another for a long time and have shared history.

Greetings and Good-Byes: Worth the Effort Every Time

Greetings and good-byes make a huge impact because even fleeting moments of connection breed feelings of belonging. Mornings can be busy. Rushing is the usual way. Taking thirty seconds to say, "Good morning," "Good-bye," "I love you," and "Have a good day" shows your teen you make them a priority. Further it lets teens know you care by giving them undivided attention at these times of acknowledgment.

Welcoming teens home after a long day is another time to connect. You don't have to question how their day went. It can just be "Welcome home. So nice to see you." When you show your teen you are happy to see them, they feel your genuine interest in being around them.

When your teen was little, bedtime was most likely a ritual of bath, story time, and cuddles. Over the years, this hands-on process fades. However, some sort of ritual is important when sending them off to bed (or maybe you head to bed first). A simple "Good night. I love you." Or you may recognize them: "I'm so proud of how kind you were to your friend today." It can also be a time of more intimate sharing.

Cuddle Time Builds Rapport

When my kids were little, we would have cuddle time. We would play the question game. They could ask me three questions about anything, and I could ask them three questions. The questions were fun and silly. We would ask everything from "What was your favorite thing to do when you were my age?" to "What's your favorite food?" to "Why is the world round?"

This was a time of cultivating connection and openness. The game created an exchange of questions and sharing. It got them in the pattern of asking me anything, sharing their thoughts and feelings, and tolerating me asking them.

My questions to them were also silly and fun. But they were mixed with other, more feeling types of questions: "How are you feeling about what happened today?" "How do you think you will feel about heading into fourth grade?"

We continued the tradition even as they grew older into their teenage years. Of course, the questions evolved. As they got older, it just became time for close conversations, and sharing progressed to more difficult topics.

Beyond connecting verbally, in these moments, you can also share affection. As in any relationship, affection shows your care and love. It brings comfort and closeness.

Just as bedtime rituals don't have to cease as your child heads into adolescence, affection shouldn't either. As discussed in chapter 1, welcome touch (hugs, kisses, and cuddling on the couch) can be emotionally regulating.

Hellos, good-byes, good nights, and good mornings are all small bids for connection yet such meaningful invitations to volley with your teen. Greetings show their value to you and convey to them the importance of your relationship. Greetings subtly say, "You matter to me, and I care about you."

Ask yourself how you show your child you are happy to see them, that they are a bright light in your day.

How do you send your teen off to go about their day?

How do you greet them when they arrive at home?

Are you saying good night?

Barriers to a Sense of Belonging

The large spectrum of behaviors families may exhibit under stress can create barriers to a teen's sense of belonging. Negative behaviors disrupt secure attachment between parents and teens. When home life is permeated by judgment, criticism, shaming, bullying, or abuse, then trust is broken. Teens disconnect when their emotional safety is compromised.

Common Barriers to Belonging

- judgment
- criticism
- shaming
- micro-offenses
- bullying
- psychological abuse
- physical abuse

Some parents frequently using the barriers to belonging might be doing so in an effort to get kids to comply without realizing how damaging these actions can be. Try to imagine your kid's friends or a stranger treating them the way you do. What would your reaction be? Unfortunately, family members often treat people outside their home better than those inside the home.

Parents may be defaulting to their experience in their own family of origin (which will be discussed in chapter 4). Other parents may not know how to emotionally regulate themselves and then unintentionally or intentionally take out frustrations on their child instead. If you have ever lost your cool or run out of ideas, resorting to almost any tactic to get your kids to behave, you are certainly not alone. Negative behaviors may present as single, unintentional episodes or as a repetitive cycle of bullying and abuse.

The overall relational climate at home—the emotional tone of the household—impacts a sense of belonging. Ideally, openness fills interactions with emotional warmth, comfort, patience, and kindness. Teens thrive in an environment of what R. F. Baumeister and M. R. Leary describe as "frequent, nonaversive interactions within an ongoing relational bond."[10] That is what promotes healthy, well-regulated teens that have a sense of belonging.

All family members' moods and communication styles contribute to the home atmosphere—parent to teen, sibling to sibling, and parent to parent. Parents take the lead in regulating an emotional climate that conveys, "You are accepted and respected, you matter, and you are welcome here."

The goal is to live in not a perfect state of perpetual happiness but rather an environment that welcomes a spectrum of honest, emotionally regulated interactions. Your kids will appreciate it if you have an awareness of your own mood, can name it and share it, and encourage them to do the same.

Bullying . . . at Home?

Bullying at home? Yes, it happens. The American Psychological Association (APA) defines bullying as "persistent threatening and aggressive physical behavior or verbal abuse directed toward other people, especially those who are younger, smaller, weaker, or in some other situation of relative disadvantage."[11]

It might be surprising to hear that some of the ways parents interact with their kids are actually bullying behaviors. Studies on parenting have come a long way, but some old, outdated ideas still exist. The dominant tendency used to be parenting by fear, shaming, casting punishment, using authoritarian power, and using aggressive means. To what end? The tactics often end up backfiring—creating defiance, resistance, and anger.

Given that parents are their teens' primary attachment figures, you can imagine the impact living in fear of one's parent(s) can have. Bullying at home has more of a damaging effect than bullying outside the home. At home, teens begin to question their worth and question the love of their parent(s). They may feel, "Something must be wrong with me that I deserve to be treated this way."

Whenever someone teases, uses sarcasm, name-calls, shames, withdraws affection, stonewalls, threatens, and yells, they are using bullying behaviors that belittle and demean. These tactics cause disconnection and psychological distress for your teen and you. Bullying damages the parent-teen relationship (in fact, any relationship) and destroys the sense of belonging at home.

Much negative behavior that happens at home is not recognized as bullying behavior. In fact, a parent may simply see it as a way of parenting. Teens' painful feelings upon being bullied are often not acknowledged or are minimized. Recovery from a parent bullying a teen can be a lifelong endeavor.

Judgment and Criticism Push Teens Away

Acceptance creates belonging; judgment (forming subjective opinions about others) is the force that pushes others away. Judgments, when spoken, become criticism. When directed at a person's character, criticism becomes shaming. All of these are barriers to connection and expressions of contempt.

Adolescence involves a lot of self-examination, so teens frequently anticipate external judgment (real or perceived) at school, online, and at home. Judgmental attitudes in general have an impact on your teen. Even if you aren't judging and criticizing your kids directly, when they witness you judging others, it makes an impact. It sends the message it's okay to tear down others; that's what everyone does. This models relational aggression, signaling that others are inferior in some way and that you don't accept them.

Teens may wonder, "Will my parent(s) judge me for my choices?" Teens tend to be self-conscious and unsure. They continually question themselves. Their biggest fears include being judged by peers. The daily internal dialogue: "Do I have the right outfit on?" "Does my acne look that bad?" "Will my friends judge me today?" "How should I act around my crush?"

Parents play a big part in how a teen will internally judge themselves (or not). Parents' acceptance reassures teens. A parent's judgment translates into teens questioning, "What do you think of me?" and "Can I be my full self and not fear being judged by you?"

Fear of judgment can lead to perfectionism. Parents' well-intentioned, natural desire to help teens grow and reach goals sometimes crosses over into constant critiquing—nitpicking, fixing, and finding fault. Humans have a negative bias and tend to see and comment on the negative more than the positive. Persistent critiques can feel judgmental and critical, taking a lasting toll on a teen's mental health. Social media already creates an illusion of perfection and impossible standards. Parental pressure only serves to "pile on."

So how can you set family standards without adding pressure? People often consider "what is acceptable" as what feels familiar and comfortable to them. Parents are no different. Society (including people you have never met), culture, religion, and our family of origin typically define what the mind thinks is acceptable. You can set family standards without adding pressure by knowing your values, modeling the behavior you want to see, and making clear requests of your teens.

Teens today have many influences and ways of finding their own identity. What they choose may not be in line with what is familiar or preferred by their parents. The unknown or unfamiliar often evokes fear. Judgment may quickly follow.

Criticism may occur if what your teen is doing looks and feels different from what you want for yourself. Criticism can serve as an attempt to control your teen's choices, but it only serves to push them away.

Examples of Critical Comments	
Behavior	**Abilities**
"You are doing that wrong."	"That's not good enough; I'll just do it myself."
"You're never going to get it right."	"This essay has no structure."
"That's not how we cut the onion!"	"Why aren't you doing more?"
"It's okay, but . . ."	"Focus!"
"Why aren't you . . . ?" "What's wrong with you?"	
Appearance	**Feelings**
"Whoa, getting a bit of a double chin."	"You have nothing to complain about."
"You sure you want to leave the house looking like that?"	"Why are you upset? It's not that big of a deal."
"Seriously, have you brushed that hair?"	"There's nothing to cry about."
	"Get over it."

Criticism isn't always verbalized. Nonverbal expressions of disapproval—usually about appearance, behavior, performance, and ideas—land heavily as criticism too.

Trying to get your teen to comply through judgment and criticism will not only backfire but also demotivate them. Constant criticism may cause them to become anxious, self-critical, and stuck in their heads. Teens' mental health benefits most from homes that provide a haven of acceptance.

Shaming Criticizes a Person's Character

Criticism shifts to shaming when it becomes a personal attack or a dig at someone's character. You may think you are giving constructive feedback when you are actually shaming.

Shaming imposes guilt and is degrading and harmful because a person's character is being criticized. An unspoken element of shaming is "When I feel shamed, it is not safe to be myself."

Examples of Shaming Comments

Behavior	Abilities
"You are a spoiled brat."	"You should _____ like your sister/brother."
"I am so tired of dealing with you."	"How could you forget _____? How stupid."
"You are a pain in my side."	"You can't ever get it together. You're just lazy."
"You are a crybaby."	
"You make my life difficult."	

Appearance	Feelings
"Are you really going to wear that?"	"Seriously, you are crying again."
"You look like you lost weight. You look better."	"You're always overreacting."
	"You're so sensitive."
"You look like you are inviting sex in that dress."	"You're such a wimp. Why can't you just suck it up?"

Even when you aren't in a disagreement, you may accidentally shame your kids by making them the butt of a joke or tease. Teasing and sarcasm can seem harmless: "Hey, I am just being funny. Don't take it so personally." But it is usually poking the bear a bit. There is sometimes a bit of truth in the joke, and it can be a passive-aggressive way of getting out what you really want to say.

Teens can also feel shame when a parent doesn't allow them to move on from their mistakes. It's easy for parents to latch onto a single error a child makes and never let them forget it. One teen got caught drinking the first time during his freshman year of high school. Every time he went out after that, his father said, "And don't be drinking again." In a family session, his son asked him, "Do you think I am just a f*** up? Will you ever let it go that I tried alcohol over a year ago?"

If siblings do the bullying, in your teen's mind, it's a reflection of you. Teens say, "I don't know why they allow my sister to treat me that way" or "Sometimes they laugh or chime in. They know it bothers me."

It might require a clear interjection on your part, such as "This is not how we treat each other in our family." If you continually model healthy relational interaction, your whole family will soon follow. It is work, but home needs to be a safe zone, free from humiliation.

Yelling Invokes Fear and Feels Chaotic

When a parent yells, it feels chaotic to kids. While you likely have endured it at some point, yelling is a form of verbal abuse. It can be painful, lonely, and scary for any child or teen. One teen described, "It feels dangerous at home. I can't concentrate; it monopolizes my thoughts."

Further, it is only a matter of time before they will be doing exactly what you are doing. Whatever behaviors you are modeling you will see reflected by your kids. In therapy, they say things like "I do anything to avoid being home. My parents yell all the time, whether it's directed at each other or me. I have started to meet them right where they are and raise my voice. Then they tell me I am disrespectful."

Verbal and emotional abuse can affect how the brain is wired and functions. Studies have shown that verbal abuse, including yelling and harsh verbal discipline, can have the same lasting effects as physical abuse.[12]

Verbal and Nonverbal Micro-offenses Damage Relations

Micro-offenses include minor slights, insults, invalidations, put-downs, and other small but offensive behaviors. Well-intentioned parents may be unaware their kids feel demeaned due to micro-offenses that take place during daily interactions.

Verbally, this might include making snide comments or acting in a condescending manner. Nonverbally, micro-offenses might involve using "air quotes," mimicking behavior, making facial expressions that exude negative messaging, or giving contemptuous looks.

Jay's Story: Little Looks and Jabs

Jay, a seventeen-year-old junior in high school, asked his parents if he could see a therapist, so they obliged. During my intake with Jay's parents, I asked what brought them to therapy. Both parents seemed puzzled about why their son wanted to seek therapy but said they were happy that he spoke up.

In my first session with Jay, he shared that he felt his mother sent him signals that he interpreted as her being annoyed with him: "I am not sure she really likes me or enjoys being around me. I seem to annoy her most of the time."

When I asked Jay what his mother was doing that gave him that impression, he said, "She gives me these looks. It's hard to describe, but it just feels negative. She also makes fun of me, like little jabs."

I asked Jay if he would be willing to have a session together with his parents. He agreed.

That session revealed that Jay's mother had no idea she was coming across this way to her son. She was upset that she had been giving her own child such negative messaging. She apologized and said she would try to catch herself. She also invited Jay to let her know when he felt this negative feeling inside.

If you catch yourself making micro-offenses or get called out for your actions, learn alternative ways to interact. Even if you feel others are being "too sensitive" at first, in time you will feel better as you learn not to accidentally offend the people around you. Any aggression (even a micro one) blocks connectedness.

Exclusion Destroys Sibling and Family Dynamics

When parents have more in common with one teen sibling than another, it can be quite apparent. This disparity in bonding can prevent connection and leave a teen feeling "less than" in some way.

Even if a parent naturally connects with one child more than others because they have common interests, parents need to make an effort to have "a special thing" with each child in the family—a special way of relating to them.

Spending time individually with each child sends the message "You all are important to me. No one is 'my favorite.'" Favoritism isn't fair and can cause psychological damage in both the short and long term.

Recognize the Range of Psychological/Emotional Abuse

The APA defines emotional or psychological abuse as nonphysical abuse, or "a pattern of behavior in which one person deliberately and repeatedly subjects another to nonphysical acts that are detrimental to behavioral and affective functioning and overall mental well-being." Forms that emotional abuse may take include "verbal abuse; intimidation and terrorization; humiliation and degradation; exploitation; harassment; rejection and withholding of affection; isolation; and excessive control."[13]

Psychological abuse stems from an imbalance of power involving someone of authority and someone in a vulnerable position. Both psychological abuse and bullying are forms of intimidation and exhibit similar repeated behaviors.

The difference between bullying and abuse has to do with frequency and severity. Conflict and disagreements can also cause distress but do not fall under bullying or psychological abuse unless the following is repeated over and over again.

The Spectrum of Abuse

accidental | unintentional | intentional | infrequent | frequent

---

Overt and covert forms of bullying and psychological abuse exist. Each creates a toxic home environment with lasting negative psychological outcomes. These tactics damage the parent-teen relationship (really any relationship) and a sense of belonging. They cause disconnection and psychological distress for you and your teen.

> Overt: yelling/screaming/shouting, cursing, insults, name-calling, threatening, humiliation, ostracizing, degrading, guilt tripping-blaming, judging, criticizing, shaming, aggression, uncontrolled anger
>
> Covert: overcontrolling, stonewalling, withholding affection, gaslighting, projection, passive-aggressive communication

It's important to note that covert forms of abuse may be more subtle. It can be difficult to say, "Yes, this is bullying or abusive" (it's hard to put your finger on what is going on, but you feel uneasy, anxious, or afraid in the environment).

Further, a longitudinal study's findings suggested, "Parental warmth is not sufficient to buffer against the detrimental effects of parent cursing, yelling, or insults which appear to be particularly psychologically damaging for the developing adolescent."[14]

Behaviors within the spectrum of bullying and psychological abuse do not work as a method of parenting. They only serve to damage a child's self-worth. They can be harmful to a teen's mental health in the short and long term. Research notes that being bullied creates changes in the stress response system and in the brain. These changes are associated with the risk of mental health problems. In addition, being bullied can compromise cognitive function and hinder one's ability to create healthy self-regulation.[15]

Bullying at home creates strain and disconnection within the parent and teen relationship. Teens may bully their peers and, in the long term, repeat the cycle in their own families.

The Ten Adverse Childhood Experiences

1. Physical abuse

2. Sexual abuse

3. Emotional abuse

4. Physical neglect

5. Emotional neglect

6. Mental illness, depressed or suicidal person in the home

7. Incarcerated relative

8. Exposure to domestic violence

9. Drug-addicted or alcoholic family member

10. Loss of a parent to death or abandonment by parental divorce[16]

Unfortunately, adverse childhood experiences (ACEs) are common. These include all types of abuse—physical, sexual, neglect, psychological, or emotional. This can be direct or witnessed. About 64 percent of US adults reported they had experienced at least one type of ACE before age eighteen, and nearly one in six (17.3 percent) reported they had experienced four or more types of ACEs.[17] Abuse happens in homes of all economic statuses, races, ethnicities, and cultures. Stress can increase incidents.

Physical Abuse Alienates and Harms with Long-Term Effects

Physical violence is the most obvious abuse. Parenting with anger and aggression prevents a sense of security and belongingness at home. Parents may use their power with the excuse "I am the parent, so I know best." This is unhealthy, unproductive, and harmful.

Many studies have confirmed that physical aggression can leave a lasting negative impact on a child's mental health. Kids who have endured physical abuse stay in fight-or-flight mode longer with long-term effects. The Centers for Disease Control and Prevention (CDC) reports that preventing ACEs could reduce the number of adults with depression by as much as 44 percent.[18]

Adverse childhood experiences in the home can inhibit trusting bonds between parent and child. Intentional or not, bullying and abuse are problems that must be addressed. Seek professional help to break cycles of bullying and abuse at home.

Avoid Self-Diagnosis and Mislabeling Behavior

In the early days of my career, I worked with elementary-aged children. I had many conversations with school staff who would jump to diagnosing attention-deficit/hyperactivity disorder (ADHD) in their students who displayed signs of hyperactivity and inability to focus in class. Teachers were not always aware of specific home life situations that were creating instability and anxiety for a child. Now there is trauma-informed training to help teachers and support staff to better be able to see how a child's behavior and mental well-being are impacted by stress and trauma at home.

Takeaway: Effective Parents Create Trust and Belonging

Trust and acceptance from a parent during the adolescent years are crucial. It impacts self-acceptance, self-worth, and even how teens function and perform in the short term and long term.

Belonging establishes the security for a healthy back-and-forth volley with your teen. A parent's judgment causes relational disconnection, and the teen quits playing or walks off the court. It's important, whether you agree or disagree with your teen, that you keep the volley going.

When looking at cultivating a sense of belonging at home, consider the overall feel of the atmosphere at home. That means interactions between you and your teen and everyone else in the family unit. Try setting as highest priorities "spending quality time together" and "sharing joy" rather than "getting things done."

Creating a sense of belonging in your home will have a direct positive effect on your teen. Teens are experiencing a time of big transitions—physically, emotionally, and cognitively. Home should be a place for decompression, a refuge from day-to-day stress. A place where your kids don't feel they have to please to gain their parents' acceptance. Show your teen unconditional acceptance. Hold expectations that are healthy, not controlling.

Without feelings of belonging, disconnection and loneliness emerge.

When each family member feels they matter, are accepted, and belong, their sense of safety and self-confidence increases, allowing them to move through life's difficulties with more ease. Feeling included at home builds a teen's sense of self and feelings of self-worth in the world.

Parents might not necessarily view certain behaviors as "barriers to a sense of belonging at home," but each of us has experiences of others' behaviors that matter to us. Ask yourself, "What might I be doing that actually creates a barrier to my teen feeling a sense of belonging?" Consider how your kids react to behaviors that you see as harmless. If they seem upset, this is an area to examine.

Parents who show acceptance and create an environment where their child feels belonging find greater success in the near and long term. Belonging at home and with one's family of origin translates into feelings of "belonging to oneself." To belong to oneself means to care for and love yourself. To feel assured that win or fail, "You've got this."

Parents are the teachers of this sense of belonging to oneself. They determine, to a large extent, how their child thinks and feels about themselves throughout life. Do your best to ensure belonging. Remember that respect begets respect. Model what you want your kid's behavior to be.

Next, in chapter 3, we'll look at communication—examining all the ways parents can keep the volley going (verbally, nonverbally, through emotional resonance, and more).

Chapter 2 Reflection: Ensuring Belonging

Ask yourself these questions about cultivating belonging:

- Do I let go of the to-do list long enough to connect?
- Are we relaxing together, just doing nothing?
- Are we experiencing joy and fun together?
- Is there laughter shared?
- Do I have a "thing" in common—a pastime or activity with my teen we enjoy doing together and can bond over?
- Is it time to create new traditions?

Ask yourself these questions about barriers to belonging:

- Am I using any of the "barriers to belonging" tactics described above with my teen—yelling, criticizing, bullying, and so on—why? Get curious.
- Am I causing distress to my teen in the way I'm parenting or communicating?
- Do I have a "growth mindset" when parenting—focusing on dynamic processes versus static outcomes?
- Do I have a need to control their behavior, and what do I hope to gain from that?

If something came up for you in reading this chapter, seeking help from a professional may be beneficial. The following chapters will provide additional support as you are parenting your teen.

CHAPTER 3

Effective Communication

Communication Skills and Beyond

"We need better communication skills" is one of the most frequent comments family members make in therapy. Parents sometimes wish for a few "bullet points" to help them achieve better communication. Quick tips might seem helpful, but they're not likely to tell the whole story of how to communicate better with teens. A lot goes on when you communicate—you're dealing with encoding and decoding messages. Even when the conversation is not a contentious one, there is a lot to manage.

Communicating involves sending and receiving messages with intention. You want the other person to know what you are thinking and how you are feeling and to truly understand your experience. Unfortunately, much of your intended messaging is not what the other person receives. Further, your messaging often goes unverified. Lack of verification in the communication process causes assumptions that create misunderstandings, difficult feelings, and otherwise avoidable conflict.

It may help to think about communicating this way:

- What message are you intending to send (about what you are thinking and feeling)?
- What messaging did the other person receive?
- Was the message you intended to send the message they received?

Parents impact teens in such a way that it affects what teens tell themselves about who they are. To a large degree, how you speak to your child creates your child's self-talk. Your voice will resound in their heads over the long term.

Parents influence how teens see themselves, how they feel about themselves (self-worth and self-esteem), how they deal with their emotions, and how they deal with life's difficulties and stress. Your kids will re-create the same patterns of interactions they experience with you now and well into the future. How you treat them affects their lifelong relationships with friends, intimate partners, and their own future family. Even the smallest shift in how you interact with your kids now can make a huge difference in their future ability to trust others, express their needs, allow others to comfort them, and find secure attachment with another.

The Goal of Good Communication Is to Feel Secure Attachment

Connectedness skills—including communication skills—create conditions that improve family relationships. The field of psychology values "secure attachment" because a child who has felt comforted in the presence of their caregivers is emotionally well regulated, resourced, and resilient.

Using the word *connectedness* evokes the potential for emotional closeness in the parent-teen relationship. It reflects the wishes teens express in therapy and in general when they say, "I want to be more *emotionally* close to my parents."

Parents of teens can use communication to continuously cultivate secure attachment and promote feelings of connectedness. Ideally, secure attachment is established with your child starting from birth. But it is never too late. You can still work to grow or maintain a secure attachment as your child grows into adolescence.

Teens Notice What You Show Them

The Mehrabian communication theory (the 55/38/7 rule) shows how clear communication requires attention to more than words. It sorts communication by three modes (nonverbal, paraverbal, verbal). There is some debate by researchers on the exact breakdown of percentages of each mode of communication. However, this viewpoint of communication helps with the overreliance on words, where most get tripped up, including parents and teens.

Parents often underestimate how their words come across to their teens. At least one study has found that parents view themselves as warmer and more supportive than

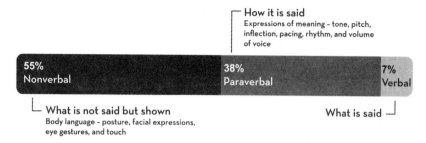

Ways we communicate

they actually are, which may explain why they often underestimate how their words affect their teens.[1] When teens express vulnerability in reaction to a parent's communication, parents often criticize the teens' reaction as "negative," further contributing to a cycle of miscommunication.

One obvious mode of communication is through verbal means. It might be shocking, but that really only accounts for about 7 percent of the messaging you are sending. Yes, words matter, but there is so much more to how people communicate.

Nonverbals account for approximately 55 percent of communication. This is your body language, posture, facial expressions, eye contact and eye gestures, and touch. For example,

> **A teen may notice, "My father won't look at me when I talk about . . ."**
> *Message sent:* no eye contact
> *Message received:* "He is ashamed of me."

Another common nonverbal is the famous eye roll. This often derails the conversation quickly between parent and teen.

Paraverbal communication accounts for around 38 percent of communication with others. This is your tone, pitch, volume, pace, rhythm, and inflection.

> **"Every time I ask my mom for help with my homework, she sighs."**
> *Message sent:* sigh
> *Message received:* "I am a bother."

Another common place we get tripped up is with the paraverbals involved in expressing "I am sorry." This can sound sincere or condescending depending on your paraverbals.

A lot of messaging flies back and forth absent of words. Teens (and all people) make meaning from these nonverbal/paraverbal signals. Teens' interpretations obviously impact their thoughts and feelings and determine how communication unfolds. When nonverbal or paraverbal signals don't match the spoken word, this sparks issues in close relationships. We tend to have less tolerance for a mismatch at home than in the world outside.

When you aren't consistent with the message you send across all modes of communication (verbal, nonverbal, and paraverbal), it can feel chaotic to teens. Teens don't know whether to trust the verbal communication when it doesn't match the other messaging they receive (or what they interpret). Unsure how to move forward, they often throw their hands up in frustration. You may hear, "Just tell me what you really want! I'm confused."

The Clear Communication Exercise

Teens and parents can communicate with each other more explicitly by looking at all the ways they are communicating—including but beyond words. Try working through each of these statements:

Your words say . . .

Your nonverbals are telling me . . .

Your paraverbals indicate to me you are . . .

If everyone is open to hearing, this exercise really helps! It works with all relationships.

Be aware that even "no communication" sends a message to your teen. Lack of communication might be received as a lack of love, a lack of caring or interest, or even disapproval. None of which may be a parent's actual intent for not communicating.

Observe What You Are Communicating About

Whether due to generational, cultural, racial, or gender-based reasons, historically, you may have received messaging that tells you, "You shouldn't talk about how you are feeling." In fact, many cultures have historically conveyed that emotions were irrational and that people who emote are "too sensitive" or "being dramatic." Yet your teen's ability to have full expression of emotions and feelings is a big part of connecting and closeness with you as their parent.

Sharing emotions is part of building trust in any relationship. Only with the details of your feelings can the other person understand your experience, gaining the needed insight to show empathy for you. Teens need their parents to create a safe space where they can talk about their deeper feelings and concerns.

"We Don't Talk like This at Home"

Obviously, I talk a lot about emotions and feelings in my work with teens. I often hear from teens, "We don't talk like this at home." I find that families talk about a lot of things, but emotions and how they are feeling usually aren't part of the conversation.

When parents provide space to allow their teen to express their emotions, teens will learn emotional regulation skills. Talking about your feelings out loud to someone else helps you identify your emotions, process them, and actually organize what might feel chaotic on the inside. It provides relief of big emotions, helping you emotionally regulate and move through difficult feelings. This obviously sets the groundwork for teens talking about deeper feelings in future relationships too.

Parents need to model expressions of emotions and feelings themselves. They need to share with their children how they feel about and deal with disappointments, the stresses of life, and their day-to-day struggles. They can even share that they are just having an off day—for no reason at all. This type of sharing does not put the onus on their teen or "adultify" them but rather normalizes conversations about feelings. This exchange of feelings serves as growth for a teen.

"We're in This Together"

On my daughter's first day of high school, she hopped out of the car and wove her way to the front doors of the school. Watching her go, I felt sad and panicked at the same time.

I went home and wrote her a letter. It said a lot of things, but the most important message was "This might get hard. Please don't ever lose sight that I am on your side."

I wanted my daughter to know that we were in this together. She was a teenager, and I was her parent, but we could still be on the same side. During challenging times, we needed to work as two people on the same team.

This letter set the tone for how we dealt with issues that came up. After reading the letter, she saw that I wasn't the enemy. She appreciated me thinking about what it might be like for her entering high school. She recognized that I had her best interests in mind, even when she didn't like what I had to say. She knew I had her back.

Teens often share that it seems no one else is experiencing their particular issue or that everyone else "has it all figured out." Many teens feel alone, assuming they are the only ones struggling. This leads teens to self-judgment about having struggles, which only makes their situation feel worse.

When parents send the message that struggling can be a natural part of everyday life, it can lessen personal judgment and open the lines of communication. Getting into the daily rhythm of talking about feelings can reduce stress, help your teen move beyond what's going on for them, and bring you closer. Let them know you are open to talking about struggles together.

Luke's Story: Opening up with His Dad

Luke's parents reached out for therapy when Luke, their fourteen-year-old son, was experiencing moments of angry outbursts. He often isolated himself in his room and seemed distant.

Luke would not open up during the first few sessions, so I asked his father to accompany him to the next session. I knew that Luke's father had dealt with depression on and off in his life. I also knew his father's sharing was the way to get Luke to open up. During the session, Luke's father described how he can feel down for no reason. He shared that he can feel trapped by his feelings and that his brain tells him things won't get better. Over time, he has come to realize that it may feel like things won't get better, but they do.

As Luke's father was sharing his experience, tears were running down Luke's face. When his father was done talking, I asked Luke, "How does it feel that your dad is opening up to you?" He said, "I know he understands me and what I am going through. I now know that I can talk to him about how I am feeling and he will listen. I feel less alone."

It was one of the most powerful sessions I have witnessed. Parents have the ability to normalize how their child feels. Luke's dad showed his relatability, which offered space for Luke to share with him. Luke and his dad came for therapy every week together. Luke learned when and how to reach for each of his parents during times of need.

Affection and Other Positive Nonverbals

While everyone was "social distancing" at the outset of the COVID-19 pandemic, you may have heard the term *skin hunger*. It is a real term, also called *touch deprivation*.

Skin is the body's largest organ. When you experience pleasant or positive touch, your body releases oxytocin—known as the "cuddle" or "bonding" hormone. Touch also releases serotonin and dopamine, additional feel-good hormones. Touch can buffer stress, reduce the release of cortisol (a stress hormone), lower heart rate, and lower blood pressure.[2]

Touch is a necessity for well-being. Babies will fail to thrive without touch. In adolescents, life without touch is associated with being stressed, anxious, and depressed.[3] Of course, the need for touch differs for each individual—think of touch on a comfort-level spectrum.

Touch Can Communicate Calm

I hug my kids a lot, but during the COVID-19 lockdowns, I made it a point to hug them at least four times a day with no exceptions. I would wake my son up in the morning with a hug, meet him in the kitchen for a lunchtime hug, give him another hug after online school, and then hug him again before he went to bed. He wasn't getting the casual hugs, pats on the back, or high fives he would otherwise encounter on a typical nonpandemic day.

Touch co-regulates and calms your teen's central nervous system. Teens need to feel their parents' affection through hugs, kisses, back rubs, pats on the back, and gentle squeezes of the hand.

Many teens and young adults have talked to me about their lack of parental affection. They say they can't remember the last time their parents hugged them. They desire loving affection from their parents but share they would feel awkward initiating a hug. Some can remember affection when they were younger and are puzzled why their parents no longer offer physical displays of affection. They describe it as feeling like their parents have rejected them in some way, and it has hindered the closeness of their relationship. They say, "I hug my friends but not my parents. It seems weird."

As I have mentioned, teens want to feel emotionally close to their parents. Part of feeling close to someone is through the expression of physical affection. Affection brings feelings of connection, warmth, and security to the relationship. It is an expression of care and love, a way to bond. Studies have shown that the more parents show affection to their teens, the more teens feel loved.[4] This feeling of being loved also impacts how conflict is felt by teens. They still know they are loved amid difficulty or discord in the relationship. And the negative fallout from conflict eases.

Affection also has been shown to increase levels of self-confidence and feelings of self-worth. This helps them relate better with you and others. When parents fulfill the biological need for affection, teens become less likely to seek out affection from others. Relationships based on a craving for touch and affection may not be the healthiest.

Remember, you set the tone for your teen's future relationships. Affection is a big part of a healthy relationship. Acts of physical affection build emotional closeness.

If Your Teen Rejects Your Affection, Become Curious and Ask Why

Were your parents not affectionate with you when you were a teen? Or is physical affection not something you do with even your spouse, your significant other, other family members, or other adults? If you are uncomfortable with physical affection, your teens may sense it and may be uncomfortable too.

Have you become uncomfortable giving affection to your kids once they hit puberty? This can be common. Parents can feel unsure of hugging when their teen starts developing, especially true for dads and daughters.

Notice when you are initiating a hug or kiss. Is it in front of their friends? Try creating daily rituals of a hug in the mornings before they leave for school and at nighttime before they go to bed. Use other forms of touch that aren't a full hug—a touch on the shoulder or arm, a pat on the back. With girls, offer to brush their hair or paint their nails. Rub your son's head when you walk by. High fives or personal/secret handshakes serve as physical connections too.

Of course, keep practicing verbal expressions of affection as well. You can always say, "I love you," "I missed you today," "I was thinking about you today," and "I am proud of you."

Know Your Communication Tendencies

Whether you have ever studied the four communication styles (or tendencies, as I call them) or not, it is worth discussing them in the context of parenting. The four basic styles of communication are passive, aggressive, passive-aggressive, and assertive (transparent). I call the assertive style *transparent* because it is a better fit when discussing teens and family dynamics.

The Four Communication Tendencies

Passive Communication

Passive communication attempts to keep the peace in the family at all costs. Parents don't communicate their own true feelings or needs. They smooth over any strife in the family, trying to avoid any conflict. Teens might feel close to these parents but at times feel unsure about who is in charge or that parents even know how to parent. Teens with parents who model passive communication may think and feel the following:

"My parents are unsure of what to do."

"My parents don't take charge; therefore, I feel I need to."

"I am not sure they have my back."

"I don't feel completely safe."

"I am not sure they care about me."

Aggressive Communication

Aggressive communication demands respect. Communication is often difficult and stressful. Adolescents in this situation vacillate between retreating and rising up against their parents' aggressive nature. Teens typically don't feel close to these parents and often fear them. Teens of parents who model aggressive communication may think and feel the following:

"My parents will never let me do that. There are no exceptions to the rules."

"They don't care if I am upset. They don't care about how I feel. It is just their way."

"I can't talk to them about how I am feeling. They will not understand."

"I am scared to call them. They're going to be so mad at me."

"I wouldn't even ask them."

"Sure hope my parents don't find out about this."

Passive-Aggressive Communication

Passive-aggressive communication confuses kids. It is hard to know what will happen during interactions. What seems okay one day isn't the next. Parents' emotions fluctuate, yet kids don't know why. There is little consistency. Teens find it hard to trust their parents or know what they should be doing (or not). Teens get anxious trying to figure out the psychological puzzle. Teens with parents who model passive-aggressive communication may think and feel the following:

"Let's see what mood my parents are in."

"I feel like I am walking on eggshells at home."

"I have no idea what they will say."

"I wish I just knew what was wrong."

"I have no idea why they are mad at me."

Transparent (Assertive) Communication

Transparent communication is supportive and comforting. Teens can express how they are feeling and what they need. When a conflict arises, families talk about it and work through it. Teens don't always get their way, but they feel heard and understood. Teens with parents who model transparent communication may think and feel the following:

"I know where I stand."

"That's not allowed, but this is, so let's do this."

"If I mess up or break the rules, they will still love me."

"I know I can call them if I get myself in a bad situation."

Your communication style may mirror that of one or both of your parents. Your teen will potentially follow suit, and future generations could as well.

Cultivating Empathetic Communication

It is difficult to communicate effectively unless you are practicing empathy. Empathetic people strive to see the other person's perspective—to understand their feelings and show compassion. It is a felt sense when someone understands your situation and "gets" your emotional experience.

Showing empathy requires only a small shift for most people. You may be surprised by the difference you see in empathy-led interactions with your teen. Your understanding can diffuse a heated situation. When your teen feels understood by you, it helps calm their emotional upheaval. It is possible to disagree and still show empathy for the other person's perspective. Think of it this way—there are no right or wrong feelings, just feelings. Sensing someone is sad and thinking or saying "You shouldn't be sad" is passing judgment. We have all been sad before. You can empathize with the feeling of sadness they are experiencing, even if you don't understand their reaction to the current situation. The more empathy you show your teen, the more empathy they will show you. Closeness in the relationship will grow.

Bobby's Story: What's behind the No?

Fourteen-year-old Bobby had mentioned to his mother, Jen, that he wanted to try out for a club baseball travel league. Jen had said no. He brought the subject up in a session with her, likely to see if I could help him find out why. As he spoke, his mom abruptly said, "I told you no already. You just don't know how to listen."

Bobby threw his head back and let out a gasp of exasperation. His mother followed suit. I said to them both, "Can we hold this moment right now? Bobby, I noticed you threw your head back and let out a noise when your mom said, 'I told you no already.' Can you tell me what is happening right now?"

He expressed being frustrated and annoyed and wanting to leave the room: "I feel like I am a bother to her." He wasn't sure if his mother understood that he didn't just want to play club baseball just because his friends were there; he was genuinely interested in the sport and really thought he would be good at it.

As Mom took in what Bobby said, I asked her if this was new information for her. She replied yes. I said, "I noticed you rolled your eyes and sighed when Bobby asked again about club baseball."

She said, "I want him to have this experience, but I am a single mom with three kids, and I don't know how I would get him to the practices so far away. Club sports are expensive, and traveling teams are costly. I feel stuck. I just don't see how I can manage it financially and with the time commitment. I guess I got mad, but really, I'm sad I can't give Bobby the experience he wants. I don't want to disappoint him. So I shut down the conversation quickly when he brought it up."

Bobby's face changed from an annoyed expression to one of empathetic softness. I asked him what was going on for him now. He said, "I had no idea what was behind her no. I get it now."

He turned to his mom. "I am sorry I was annoyed with you. I had no idea why you said no and assumed you thought it was stupid that I wanted to try out. I also assumed you thought I wasn't good enough. I can clean windows to make some money to help pay. I can also catch a ride with teammates to practice."

She replied, "I'm sorry I got mad and didn't explain why I said no. I can see why that was confusing for you. No, I don't think it is stupid at all. I'm happy you're thinking about exploring something new. I do think you are good enough to make the team."

Their nonverbal responses in the first thirty seconds derailed the entire conversation, leading to disconnection. Neither parent nor teen felt heard, understood, or validated in their experience. They also created internal thoughts and feelings that went unverified, causing incorrect assumptions of what the other was thinking and feeling.

Slowing things down is key. You are better able to notice what's happening for yourself internally and gain a real understanding of what's happening between you and your teen as the interaction unfolds. Processing thoughts and feeling out loud helps you both understand each other's position. This helps the relationship feel open, leading to transparency—and less conflict.

Bobby's story continues in chapter 6.

When you show your children empathy, they learn how to be empathetic themselves. The skill of empathy helps people create personal and professional social connections and can directly impact the success of intimate relationships as well. Strong emotional bonds lead to long-lasting relationships and overall happiness.

Develop Mutual Understanding with Your Teen in Three Steps

Parents can facilitate greater understanding with teens in a few ways. Rather than simply reacting to what a teen says, you can slow down by taking these steps: notice, listen, and respond.

Notice: What's Happening When You Communicate?

Notice that many messages are being sent during a parent-teen interaction. You're processing a lot of signals both "within" yourself and "between" yourself and your teen when you try to communicate. It helps to step back from the content of the message and notice what else is happening.

Focus on your internal experience in the present moment: you may find a mix of physical sensations, thoughts, feelings, and action tendencies. Some people know immediately how they feel during an argument with their teen. They might say "My chest is on fire" or "My throat is tight." Unfortunately, many people don't slow down to notice their body signals. When asked "What is going on in your body?" they simply don't know. Chapter 5 shares more about how to learn to use your body to facilitate better communication.

Second, you can recognize your own filters, patterns, and self-narratives. Perhaps you will even begin to recognize some of your own cognitive distortions—faulty or inaccurate thoughts, perceptions, or beliefs. Look within yourself as difficult feelings arise or conflict emerges. This provides you the chance to examine what you may not have noticed before. How are you blocking their point of view? How are they blocking yours? Chapters 4 and 5 lead you through a process of self-reflection to increase clarity and help you avoid previously unseen blocks.

Once you've slowed down to notice a more complete picture of what might be happening during parent-teen interactions, you'll be better positioned to communicate in a healthy and emotionally regulated way.

Listen: How Can You Be a Better Listener?

When kids are little, they constantly say, "Watch me! Look at me!" As they become teenagers, their request (expressed or unspoken) becomes "Listen to me! Listen to me!"

When you think about communication, you may think of talking, but communication is really about listening—listening to understand! On one hand, you may feel your teen doesn't listen to you. On the other, a frequent comment from teens is that they feel their parents don't listen to them. It is a two-way understanding. Parents modeling and leading with solid listening skills helps teens listen to understand parents as well.

The skill of listening is critically important in cultivating connectedness in the parent-teen relationship. Everyone wants someone to listen—to both problems and good news. Parents and teens are alike in this regard.

Teens want their parents to hear their opinions, the latest gossip, the tragedy of the morning blemish, the fact they have no clothes to wear, the privilege they desire next, or their personal problems, but really, they only want their parents to listen. All the above is filled with your teen's feelings, of course.

Taking the time to just listen is so important. No agenda in mind and no parent hat on either. Just mom/dad listening.

An Empathetic Ear

I remember sitting in my oldest daughter's room listening to her share about the difficulties she was having with her friend groups, guys, and life in general. Even though she was sharing her worries and insecurities, I enjoyed the opportunity to learn about her world! I was conscious of only listening and not interjecting my opinion or my take on the situation.

Sometimes she just needed time to vent with someone who would listen and provide an empathetic ear. I was happy to be one of the lucky ones she trusted as she spilled the contents of the day.

If you can simply listen with an open mind during your teen's venting, you will become better prepared to listen during times of distress. Teens experience many worrisome times, even when life is otherwise relatively calm. When your teen wants to share, see it as a compliment. They trust you enough to open up.

Teens also want to feel that their parents understand them or at least make an effort to really try. That's not asking much because everyone wants to be understood. Understanding someone takes time and patience. No one wants to be rushed when they are trying to tell you how they are feeling.

Be curious to gain an understanding of what they are going through. Try saying, "Can you explain more so I can understand?" When you come from the angle of communicating to gain an understanding of the other person's experience both situationally and emotionally, the conversation goes much differently. Often most are interested in getting their point across, telling a teen what to do, being right, or winning the conversation. That's human nature. Yet this approach to communicating causes more emotional disconnection than connection. "Winning" really gets you nowhere when communicating, as you'll see below in "Identifying Barriers to Effective Communication."

Respond: Confirm, Empathize, and Validate

As mentioned above, the messages intended to be sent aren't always the ones received. Confirming what you are hearing the other person saying is vitally important to keep communication on track and avoid misunderstandings and disconnection. Confirm by paraphrasing what you hear them say. This helps them know you're engaged and really getting them. When someone feels understood, it calms escalated feelings and diffuses arguments. Try asking, "My understanding is that you feel _____. Is that right?" or "I hear you saying _____. Is that right?"

Empathizing with your teen shows them you understand. It's how they know you genuinely care about them and their situation, regardless of the issue's size or scope. Empathy is putting yourself in your teen's shoes. An expression of empathy, validation literally means you indicate that you see their feelings as "valid."

To validate, share with your teen that you hear them, how they are feeling makes sense, and you "get" their experience. Make it explicit. Say things like "I hear you are feeling sad," "I would be sad if that were happening to me," and "That sounds hard. I understand why you are frustrated. I would be frustrated too."

It's easy to tell when someone is actually listening or not, isn't it? But it's harder to tell if they understand your perspective (even if they don't agree). That is why the validation of a parent is so important. By being responsive and validating your teen, you show engagement and express how much you want to hear and understand them. Understanding calms and helps regulate the nervous system; validation brings comfort and reassurance. Your teen knows you really get them when you remain open-minded.

It is also a good time to normalize what your teen is experiencing with comments like "I hear you are scared about making the transition to college. It is a big step. It's not just you; most people are nervous." It's reassuring to hear from a parent that "It's okay to feel the way you are feeling. You aren't alone."

Parents can also show their vulnerability, too, by saying things like "I had a hard time when I graduated college. I felt a bit lost." Just try to keep the focus on your teen's experience.

In a routine conversational exchange, each person typically spends an equal amount of time listening to the other person (50 percent listening, 50 percent talking). However, if you recognize that your teen just needs to be heard, experiment with listening for more than 70 percent of the conversation. The remaining portion of the time you can spend confirming, empathizing, and validating.

Nonverbals also need to be communicating that you are listening. Put away the distractions, including your phone! Have an attentive and open body posture. Making eye contact also signals you are present and can enhance emotional connection.

Own and Repair: What Often Gets Missed

Watching fouls called in an NBA game feels quite like what happens in close relationships during conflict: looks of outrage, arguing, defending, and hands thrown back, basically saying, "Who me? I didn't do that!"

Many can relate to the experience of being in a relationship with someone who doesn't take responsibility for their actions—who deflects and defends. It can be a continual rupture in the relationship. Owning your stuff can get a bit more complicated with the parent-child relationship. It is about power: "I'm the authority figure. I demand you respect me." Of course, you've likely noticed that demanding respect isn't how to get it. Respect begets respect.

Parents often feel their child will not see them as the authority figure or will lose respect for them if they take ownership. But it actually has the opposite effect. Teens share that they lose respect for their parents when the parent doesn't admit being a part of the reason their communication goes sideways (when they have yelled, called their teen names, or simply not taken the time to listen). Teens also express losing respect when a parent uses their position of power instead of being open to a discussion or explaining why they are making a decision. Think of the statement "Because I said so."

An interaction gone bad is rarely always one person's fault. Parents verbalizing ownership of their missteps, whether during an interaction that was filled with conflict or not, sends the message that parents are willing to see their own misgivings. They are willing to hear when they hurt feelings or didn't handle a situation as well as they could have. It shows introspection and self-awareness. It shows honesty and vulnerability. It builds trust and emotional connection. It speaks to "I am invested in this relationship with you and willing to look at myself." And it is good modeling! In any relationship, thinking you wouldn't ever hurt someone's feelings is unrealistic.

Owning is only part of the repair. Teens share that they don't understand why their parents won't just say, "I am sorry." Parents need to take the next step, saying sorry for their part in the interaction going south.

Saying "I am sorry" doesn't mean that you were wrong in your position, such as telling your teen they couldn't go to the party. Instead, an apology says you could have dealt with telling them in a better way.

The question of sincerity is also key in any apology. "Sorry you made me mad and I yelled" isn't a real apology. Sincerity sounds more like "I lost my temper. I was frustrated, and I lashed out, calling you a spoiled brat. I shouldn't have done that. I am sorry I hurt your feelings" or "I was overwhelmed, and I didn't know how to handle what was happening. I am sorry."

An apology shows you care about them, their feelings, and the relationship. When you show your teens that you own your part and apologize, they will do the same.

Process an apology out loud. You can say, "I realized I was being short with you. My tone was harsh when I said, 'Why did you do that?' Then I realized I shouldn't have blurted that out, and I laughed to make light of what I said. I realized you then thought I was laughing at you. That wasn't my intention. I am sorry for hurting your feelings."

If you think about it, acknowledging the other person's feelings and apologizing when you hurt them is a part of any healthy relationship. Why should it be different in the parent-teen relationship?

Identifying Barriers to Effective Communication

Effective parent-teen communication is reciprocally voiced, heard, validated, and responsive. It is conveyed with sensitivity to emotional states. A barrier to effective communication is anything that may be preventing this safe exchange from happening. Removing even one barrier can go a long way toward making positive shifts in how you and your teen communicate.

Negative Patterns of Communication Can Cause Disconnection

As indicated, a lot goes on when you communicate—both within yourself and between you and your teen. When someone gets flooded with emotion, it can feel overwhelming and cloud effective communication. You or your teen may lose your cool and resort to unhealthy communication tactics. When your emotions get the best of you, communication can go off track—moving you away from how you want to be with your teen.

Kids don't do what you say; they do what you do. Parents are human too. Modeling good communication skills brings some pressure. Yet you can't expect something from your kids that you aren't doing yourself. Stay open-minded. The better you are at communicating, the better your teen will be.

Alongside cultivating effective communication, looking out for barriers to healthy communication with your teen is important to prevent disconnection. The following are common causes of disconnection between parent and teen (and in all our relationships).

Problem-Solving Sounds Useful but Actually Backfires with Teens

One of the most common communication problems is quickly jumping to solving the other person's dilemma and not really listening. Parents can easily get caught in this trap with their teen. The teen may say, "You are more interested in fixing me than hearing how I am feeling!"

Parents have good intentions when they are focused on solving their child's distress. They see their kid faced with a difficult situation and witness their suffering. Parents hurt when they see their kid in pain. However, the solution to calming their suffering is listening.

When you jump to solving a situation without listening first, you send the message that you know better. Problem-solving implies you need to tell them what to do to fix the situation and "them." This can send a teen into a place where they feel cut off emotionally. They will likely end the conversation, throw up their hands, and say, "You don't even want to hear how I am feeling. You don't care."

It is best to try to jump into their emotional experience rather than jumping to solve. You might even try asking, "Is this a time you want me to listen or a time you want me to problem-solve with you?"

You may need to take a few deep breaths to calm yourself. Stay focused on what they are sharing. Get curious, ask questions, empathize, and validate how they are feeling. This doesn't mean that after listening, you won't end up "problem-solving" with them. After listening, you can ask, "Do you want me to help solve this problem with you?"

Defending Creates a Win/Loss Atmosphere Where Everyone Loses

When communicating it is common to enter defense mode right off the bat—even when the conversation isn't a contentious one. It is nearly impossible for either person to listen well with "dukes up" in opposition. When defending, most are merely waiting for breaks in the conversation to make their point or interrupt. Some reasons to defend: "I feel threatened in some way, so I must defend" or "It's not my fault."

Parents often instinctively jump to defend themselves when they subconsciously want to let their teen know *they* aren't the ones to blame for how their teen feels. It hurts to think your teen may think their difficult feelings are because of you, so you may jump to defend mode.

When I see teens explain to their parents how they are feeling, often parents jump to "I told you" or "I was doing the best I could." The threat to the parent is being seen as a bad parent.

Defending is even more hurtful when accompanied by criticism. When words are said that can't be taken back, the result can have a lasting sting. Defensive criticism sounds like "I am doing the best I can! You are just being a spoiled brat."

Any of us may move quickly into defense to avoid hearing something negative about ourselves. Attempting to avoid uncomfortable feelings is natural. You may even feel the threat of "being in trouble"—as when you were a child. If you can catch yourself, you can help your teen do the same.

The trouble is when focusing on your position, you do not gain an understanding of the other person's experience. The message is "I am more concerned about defending my position than hearing you."

When this kind of communication takes you away from understanding each other, each person can lose their sense of psychological safety. Meaning one or both people in a conversation feel the need to hold back because they feel unsafe to share. They can't express their true thoughts and feelings. No one gets their message across, and both people leave feeling unsatisfied with the communication.

Deflecting and Displacing Blame Won't Work

Deflecting during conflict is common, especially for those who have a hard time saying, "Okay, that's on me. I am sorry." This again can get tricky with the parent-teen relationship. Parents don't want to lose their authority. However, it can't always be 100 percent someone's fault in any relationship. Teens often ask, "Why is it always all on me?" It can contribute to the perpetual feeling of being in trouble.

Teens can more easily take ownership of their part (and not deflect it back to you) when you do the same. When a parent accepts even a small part, like their tone of voice turning a communication worse, it can feel better than a refusal to own any of it.

Parents have a lot of responsibilities, which come with a lot of stress. Teens usually don't really understand how stressful it is to pay the bills, work a full-time job, try to make your boss happy, and accomplish all that is entailed in being a parent. Why? They haven't had the experience yet. They also are developmentally in a place where they feel the world revolves around them. Teens are naturally a bit self-centered. Not in a bad way—just as a symptom of their current stage of development.

Teens also have stress and have less capability of dealing with the same level of stress as adults. Parents and teens undoubtedly are overwhelmed and exhausted when they arrive home. When anyone is stressed and wiped out from the day, tensions can be high. The outcome can be displacing our unpleasant feelings on someone else, "throwing our emotional mud." Both parents and teens often say, "I feel like they take out their stress on me."

Uncomfortable feelings need to go somewhere, and it is common to throw them around like mud. However, spewing anger surely won't allow either of you to feel open to healthy communication. It can ignite emotional dysregulation in the household, causing disconnection.

Simply stating "I feel off today; it's not about you at all," "I had a bad day and am feeling edgy," "I am not in a good mental space and need a bit of quiet time," or anything that allows you each to know how the other is doing can relieve tension and prevent conflict.

Criticism and Contempt Only Serve to Push People Away

Criticism can erode any good relationship. It keeps the other person at a distance. Just as criticism can hinder your teen's sense of belonging, it also creates a barrier to healthy communication. You may have memories of hearing comments growing up that you would never want to or intentionally say to your kids. Things like "That was so stupid, why did you do that?" "I think you need to cut down on the food," "That outfit makes your stomach look larger, you should change," "If you don't make good grades you won't amount to anything," or "Seriously, why can't you get it right?" The safety of closeness is jeopardized with critical statements like these.

Over the years, recognizing what is appropriate to say and what not to say has become clearer. Language and meanings evolve and adapt over time. You don't hear someone with a disability being called "crippled" any longer. Similarly, society is growing aware of problematic terms such as *crazy* and *normal*. Critical statements can be damaging to any relationship. Some people brush off the significance of word choice by calling the person on the receiving end "sensitive," but this endangers a relationship.

As noted earlier, teens perceive much of their interaction with their parents as negative. The "You should . . . You haven't . . . You need to . . ." conversations are meant to keep kids on track but can land as being critical to a teen and cause conflict.

Even if you think you are dishing out positives to your teen, check in with them about how the balance feels to them. Humans tend to filter out positives and only hear negatives. It's called mental filtering. For this reason, among others, parents must consciously, explicitly, and repeatedly express to teens positive feedback. Share the whole picture of how you feel about them.

No one is perfect, and every parent and child say and do things that land critically with each other. Sometimes you really just can't hear the criticism in what you say. Frankly, it doesn't matter if you hear it; they do. Say something like "I didn't realize that came across as critical; I am sorry. My intention is never to hurt your feelings." Apologize if a comment lands poorly, even if you disagree that the statement sounded critical or it wasn't your intention to criticize. Teens will follow your lead.

Teens take parents' comments to create much of their own self-narrative, which impacts their self-esteem and self-worth now and throughout life. Criticism—even when a parent isn't in conflict with a teen—can hit them hard. It prevents them from sharing things with you for fear of a critical response. If the goal is for your kids to feel connectedness within your relationship, criticism is the antithesis of connectedness.

Avoiding and Withdrawing Represent Attempts to Escape Pressure

Avoiding or withdrawing are common ways to cope with distress. When communication is stressful, is filled with uncomfortable emotions, or feels unsafe, physically checking out—leaving the room or avoiding being in close proximity to others—or emotionally checking out are ways to escape.

The strategies of avoiding and withdrawing tend to arise when you don't see another way to deal with the situation at hand. These tactics represent a conscious or unconscious effort to survive and protect oneself in the current situation. Maybe even to protect the relationship.

Teens may get in trouble for being disrespectful when fleeing during conflict. They may not know what to do. If they cannot handle the emotional pressure, they feel the need to escape. Maybe you can relate.

Stonewalling Attempts to Manipulate Emotional States

Stonewalling is a way to avoid and withdraw from the situation; however, it is a bit more manipulative in nature. It's when you freeze out or give someone the cold shoulder or silent treatment. You are withdrawing your emotional presence but with intention.

This can be perceived as a punishment, bullying, a power play, or even a psychologically damaging tactic of communicating. Low anger may accompany snide comments, words spoken under the breath, and refusal to answer questions. It can increase the other person's anxiety or anger and hinder a secure attachment.

When parents stonewall teens, it is usually after a teen has done something their parent isn't too pleased about. Teens often say when they get in trouble, the situation can linger for days. They may say, "I made a mistake. I genuinely apologized, but my mom/dad can't get past it." It can be difficult for a teen to handle a parent's emotional withdrawal due to their missteps.

Teens stonewall too. "I know something is wrong, but they won't tell me." Parents may feel shut out by their teen. Giving a teen their privacy is needed, but being in the know when something is really wrong is important. However, teens may not know themselves what's wrong. They may be stonewalling simply because they don't know how to process or articulate their feelings. Stonewalling for a teen may simply be in an effort to cope with their overwhelming feelings. Another reason to create safety in expression and regularly talk about your feelings at home.

Projecting Feelings onto Your Teen Yields Poor Long-Term Effects

We all have unresolved relational wounds, insecurities, and self-judgment. When these experiences and painful feelings go unprocessed, they may result in projection, displacing one's feelings onto another. This is a common defense mechanism used to avoid uncomfortable feelings and can cause much discord in relationships. Keep in mind these defenses may be unintentional, habitual patterns of self-protection.

For parents, projection of feelings onto a teen can be a way to deal with the parent's own unacknowledged and unresolved fears, worries, and past hurts. For example, if a parent's ambition was to be an exceptional baseball player, and they experienced distressful feelings for not reaching their goal, they may pressure their teen to be the best first basemen. This can create much conflict between parent and teen: "I am just not enough for you. I am a disappointment." This can result in not only conflict but also unconsciously shaping the identity of your teen.

A parent's inner conflict might be the source of the unconscious projection, but the intention is most likely to protect their teen from experiencing similar pain.

Much misunderstanding, frustration, and conflict can occur with projection. Parents being in tune with their own feelings and past injuries is important, asking themselves, "Is this my stuff coming up or actually my teen's current experience and how they are feeling?"

Making Assumptions and Piling on Indicate the Need for a Fresh Slate

When an argument is sparked, anger can get the best of anyone, and "piling on" the other person can result. This means bringing up past arguments, mistakes, or hurts. It can also mean adding other unrelated stuff to the current discussion. The pattern of "piling on" is common in all relationships but can feel a little different for teens. Parents have a long history with their teens. They remember times when their teen got in trouble and instances where there has been a lack of maturity shown.

Teens express that sometimes parents pile on their past mistakes and don't see their growth and maturity. They say things like "Sometimes I feel my mom still views me as a middle schooler. She keeps bringing up that I cheated on one test in the sixth grade. That was three years ago! I don't do that anymore."

There is a saying that past behavior is indicative of future behavior. However, that doesn't always apply to teens because they are still in the process of maturing. You can't always make assumptions about what they are doing based on past behavior.

Teens will say "You always assume the worst of me" when talking to parents. If you assume the worst of your kids, they end up feeling bad about themselves. Teens then stoop to anger and negativity in moments of frustration. They may think, "I am already seen as bad, so just f*** it, I'll do it."

Avoid negative assumptions and give the benefit of the doubt. Teens are changing rapidly, and they may surprise you in a positive way.

How to Prevent Disconnection, Even during Discipline

When kids do things outside established rules and boundaries, it can cause much discord—leading to disconnection between parent and teen. Working through any difficult situation together will result in a better outcome if you can stay connected.

A close and connected relational foundation will only benefit you during times of discipline. Trust built between you and your teen positively impacts the discussion. When teens trust you, deep down, they know you act in their best interest. They will respect you and your decisions concerning their missteps.

Think about when you don't respect your boss at work. You basically discount what they say and tune them out. If you have a good relationship with your boss—meaning they listen to you, value your opinion, try to understand, and share a mutual respect—you wouldn't want to tell them to "f*** off."

Remind yourself that your teen may have done something wrong simply because they still have a developing brain. They often do things without considering the outcome, and they can be quite impulsive. A teenager's actions reflect their developmental stage. Think of a toddler trying to run across the street. Toddlers are not thinking of the consequences of getting hit by a car. They just want whatever is on the other side of the street.

View discipline as "teachable moments" with back-and-forth dialogue. It's not just lecturing. When faced with any difficult situation, the best way through is to take the time to talk calmly. Using anger only elevates the situation. When one person's nervous system is regulated and resourced, it invites co-regulation with another person. Imagine how an internal experience of safety would impact the outcome.

The rules of good listening apply even when disciplining. Go slow, letting both parent and teen share without interruption. Be curious and ask questions, not in an interrogating way but in an effort to better understand your teen's thought processes.

Process your emotions and feelings out loud. The teen will follow your lead. If a teen says they don't know why they did whatever they did, it may be true.

Often, teens will say in therapy, "I have no idea why I listened to my friend and did _____. I guess I got caught up in the moment and didn't think." Again, this is no surprise considering what's going on in the teenage brain. Make sure they know even when they are in trouble, you still love them.

Risky Business: Getting through Poor Decisions Together

When my son was a sophomore in high school, his father went out of town. My son decided to invite a few people over.

Not long after that, a neighbor called me to alert me of a party at the house. I jumped in the car and drove over. As I approached, I saw my son running around in a panic. When he saw me, his head dropped, and all the color left his face.

I decided to listen first before reacting. I walked up to him, calmly asking, "What happened?" He told me he had invited a few friends over, but due to social media sharing, it got out of hand. People just kept showing up. He couldn't control the situation. I asked why he didn't call me for help. He just put his head down again.

I said, "This isn't okay, but we will get through this." He exhibited shockingly poor judgment. He didn't have the forward-thinking to understand what could happen. Luckily there weren't serious consequences—other than my own.

My biggest concern, after clearing out the party, was that he didn't call me for help after realizing he had made poor judgment in his decision. It was a moment to show him that's what I'm here for—to help him when things get overwhelming.

Teens will mess up over and over just like adults do. How you react when they mess up impacts your relationship. Whether they feel comfortable continuing to reach out to you will influence their ability to deal with future mistakes.

You will find it counterproductive for teens to feel like they need to hide, lie, or be ashamed about a mistake. You want them to reach out to you. That doesn't mean accepting poor choices. Actions have consequences. Inviting people over when they aren't supposed to is not okay.

Takeaway: Communication Runs Deep

Generally, communication involves much more than you see on the surface. It may be deceiving to think that "a few quick tips to improve communication" could serve you and your teen well. Instead, if you invest small daily efforts into communicating with greater empathy, you can create lasting affection and a secure bond between you and your teen.

Working toward openness and transparent communication often requires welcoming tough emotions before reaching the feel-good ones. The goal of open communication is for your teens to share how they are feeling with you; this brings closeness. Open communication is also needed for your kids to feel safe to come to you when they are struggling or at a decision crossroads. Teens can be impulsive, but they are driven by belonging—and that can cause them to make bad decisions as well as good ones. You want them to reach out to you to learn the difference.

Understand that harsh, rules-focused communication or lecturing does not cultivate closeness in the relationship. Focus on how both the content and style of your communication could be impacting the exchange. Become cognizant of all the ways you send messages to your teen—verbally, nonverbally, and paraverbally. Recognize the many invisible barriers (unconscious protective response patterns) that may be creating noise around your efforts to listen.

You have read about the components of the volley that bring attunement to your teen's emotional state and support healthy communication: noticing signals both within yourself and your teens, listening to understand, confirming messages received, empathizing, and validating. And when there are hurt feelings or conflicts, owning and repairing can bring comfort and calm to your teen.

You also now know the barriers that frequently interrupt the volley (or get you off track with your teen). The back-and-forth volley between parent and teen brings trust and security to the relationship. By slowing things down and "volleying back" with questions to learn more, you can de-escalate conflicts.

It's not about being a perfect parent or communication with your teen being free from disagreement. It's about gaining awareness of and acknowledging your tendencies, owning them, and understanding how they may affect others. If a negative communication pattern flares up and someone's feelings get hurt, you can begin to repair the relationship with a genuine apology. Your teen will follow your example!

In chapter 4, you will self-reflect on past experiences. You may be surprised to see the extent to which life experiences inform how a person thinks, feels, and acts.

Chapter 3 Reflection: Your Communication

Ask yourself these questions about how you communicate:

- What are my communication tendencies when interacting with my teen (verbally, nonverbally, paraverbally)?

- Am I comfortable expressing my feelings?
- Am I comfortable with showing affection?
- Am I comfortable with showing empathy?
- Is there anything I am doing that will prevent my teen from coming to me to talk about how they are feeling or when they are struggling?
- What are my self-practices of coping (resourcing) when getting stuck in communicating with my teen?

CHAPTER 4

Self-Reflection on Your Past

Healthy Relationships Prioritize Self-Reflection

Humans are relational, and being in relation with one another touches every aspect of our lives. Therefore, improving our relationships for the better is our most important endeavor.

Teens are moving through new developmental stages. Parents' relationship with their teen needs to evolve with their changes in mind. Teens will have new fears, insecurities, and daily challenges to overcome while dealing with physical, social, and emotional transitions. Your relationship is the most important factor in how they manage.

If the goal is connectedness in your relationship with your teen, you must be able to self-reflect bravely. That means looking at your history alongside moment-to-moment interactions now. It requires reflecting on how your past experiences impact how you are with your teen today.

Self-Reflection Shows Your Teen You Care

Evolving is a lifelong journey, and self-reflection is an essential component. In any relationship, self-reflection shows the other person you care about them and the relationship. It indicates that you are willing to look at yourself for the betterment of the relationship.

The more aware you are of your past and your patterns, the more you can make conscious choices going forward. The past doesn't have to predict the future, nor does any past experience excuse any specific behavior in the present (meaning this is not about blaming your own parents or ancestors). The past may hold important clues to help you relate better with your teen now, at a formative time in their lives.

Self-Reflection Moves Everyone Forward

Often adults don't partake in self-reflection due to their busy lives . . . but also because looking deeply into the past can be painful. Self-reflecting can bring old wounds to the surface.

Humans tend to suppress what is too painful to deal with at the time. Even though you may try your best to ignore these hurts, they eventually reappear in some form, and it's often not pleasant. When left to fester, wounding that has not been dealt with tends to ooze or seep out. This is especially true during interactions with those who know you best, including your teens.

Self-reflection is a vehicle for forward movement. Yet self-reflection without self-compassion will result in you being stuck in a self-condemning loop. Please know, bravely self-reflecting also means being kind to yourself during the process. How can you move forward if you are held back by your own judgment? Give yourself time, space, and grace.

Reflecting on Your Past (Where Patterns Originate)

As mentioned, parents are the builders of the scaffolding that supports not only how teens feel about themselves but also how they will be in their future relationships. Parents must be willing to self-reflect to build the structure. That means self-reflection of your own thoughts, feelings, and behaviors (patterns) every day.

It makes the most sense to begin self-reflecting on *the scaffolding your parents built for you.*

Reflecting on Attachment Theory

Your attachment style is an internal working model of what you expect when relating to another person (all interpersonal relationships). The early years with your parent(s) largely created this internal working model. This includes what themes you associate with yourself (view of self) and others (view of others) within any dyad. It answers the questions "Can I and how do I express my emotions?" "What emotions are safe to

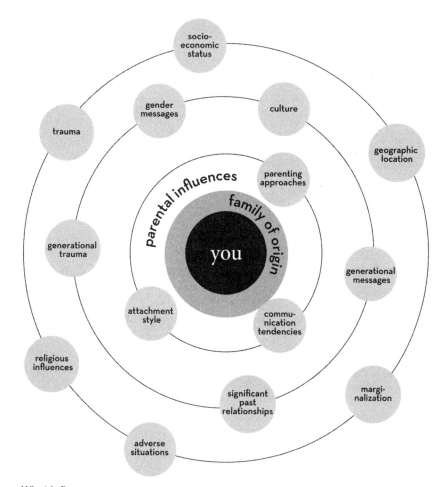

What influences you

share?" "Is it okay to have needs, and how do I express them?" "Can I count on others to reassure and comfort me?" "Can I be trusting in my close relationships?" and "Will relationships bring feelings of insecurity, fear, and rejection?" Attachment style determines whether relationships are a haven for you or not.

There are four primary attachment styles: secure, anxious, avoidant, and disorganized.[1] As mentioned in the first chapter, relationships from birth to around seven years shape development of attachment styles. However, these are not static; they can change over time depending on one's relational experiences.

Looking at attachment styles through the lens of a child, below are descriptions of the four attachment styles and what they typically feel like to a child in a relationship with their parent(s). Which feels like *your* experience growing up?

Secure Attachment

Felt experience in your relationship with your parent(s) or caregiver(s):

> Safe, stable, feelings of warmth, closeness, and parental presence
> *"My parent(s) took care of both my physical and my emotional needs."*

It was acceptable to express emotions, feelings, and needs. When you shared your feelings and needs, it was met with reassurance and comfort, meaning your parent(s) were in tune with your emotional states. Closeness felt good. Home felt safe and like a stable landing place. There were clear and realistic boundaries. You felt like a priority.

Anxious Attachment (Preoccupied)

Felt experience in your relationship with your parent(s) or caregiver(s):

> Instability, confusion, loneliness at times
> *"My parent(s) met my physical needs. Yet I felt unsure of what behavior to expect from my parent(s) and whether they would meet my emotional needs."*

Your parent(s) could be responsive, attuned, and emotionally sensitive. Other times, they could be unavailable, misattuned, and insensitive. This inconsistency in how your parent(s) related to you created a home environment that felt chaotic. Sometimes, it felt like you were attending to your parents' needs more than them attending to yours. They seemed overly involved or intrusive in your life and may have hyperfocused on your appearance and or performance.

Avoidant Attachment (Dismissive)

Felt experience in your relationship with your parent(s) or caregiver(s):

Disregarded, rejected, alone

"My parent(s) met my basic physical needs but were not attuned to my emotional needs."

Emotional closeness was difficult due to your parent(s) being distant, emotionally unavailable, and even possibly cold. You had to take care of or suppress your own emotional needs. Your parent(s) were focused on you being independent and less reliant on them.

Disorganized Attachment (Fearful Avoidant)

Felt experience in your relationship with your parent(s) or caregiver(s):

Fearful, rejected, alone

"My parent(s) was (were) not only unreliable in meeting my physical and emotional needs; I also feared them."

Your environment was inconsistent, unpredictable, and possibly traumatic. You were not able to trust your parent(s). Closeness didn't feel safe and was associated with hurt.

Exercise: Processing Your Experience

This might be a good time to write your feelings down about your own experience growing up.

Consider these prompts:

Felt sense: What was your overall "felt sense" about your relationship with your parents growing up? What did the atmosphere at home feel like?

Feelings: How do you think your parents felt about you? How did they
let you know?

Expression: Were you able to express your feelings and needs?

Comfort: Were your parents a sense of comfort for you? How did
they comfort you?

If difficult feelings arise as you reflect on these questions or read the
attachment descriptions, please take some time and space for
yourself. Seek support as needed.

When needs are unmet or the environment feels unsafe, children will inevitably create ways to cope—and this is, in part, how attachment styles develop. Defenses grow in an unconscious effort to protect the self from painful feelings like shame, guilt, uncertainty, and fear. The child creates an organized strategy to keep distress at bay. Even though it can be painful for a child to not feel safe in their relationship with their parent, rejection from a parent feels worse.

Children completely rely on their parent(s) to meet their physical and emotional needs. As a child you cannot choose to leave the relationship with your parents. Parenting with insecure attachment styles (anxious, avoidant, disorganized) can compromise a child's safety in expressing needs and feelings. (The next chapter looks deeper into defenses used to cope, including mind-body reactions.)

Trevor's Story: The Legacy of Avoidant Attachment

"My daughter is emotional, and I don't know how to deal with her. Can you teach her some coping skills?" expressed Trevor during an intake for his thirteen-year-old daughter, Ellie.

I spent half the session listening and asking questions about Ellie's current situation and past details of her life.

Then I asked Trevor about his experience growing up. He shared that his parents were wonderful, supportive, and kind to him. As I asked more questions, I learned that both his parents were emotionally absent. Trevor recalled memories of his mother lying in bed during the day hours. He would have to get himself up and fed before school. He was required to make his lunch and wake up his mother to say good-bye before he left for the bus. This routine began at the age of six.

Trevor's father traveled a lot. When he was home, he was emotionally distant. He only showed anger at times when conflict occurred. When Trevor reached for emotional support, his parents would either ignore him or change the subject. They did not initiate any conversations about emotions, feelings, or anything deep. The relationship was largely about fulfilling his basic physical and financial needs.

He was now trying to parent a teenager who was sharing many feelings, and he felt himself shutting down. He would intentionally avoid her for fear that she would need him in an emotional capacity. When they would get into arguments, he did not make an effort to resolve them because the distance felt better than the closeness. He was worried that he was pushing his daughter away as he had in previous relationships when someone tried to get emotionally close. He didn't want to do that with his daughter.

Often teens are the "identified patient." Parents come in with loving and good intentions of getting their teens help. However, just like young children, teens react to their surroundings and may not have the language to explain what's happening. In Ellie's case, she was reaching out to her father for emotional support. When he was unable to respond with comfort and reassurance, her emotions escalated. This only drove her father to create more distance between the two of them. They were both left feeling alone. The treatment needed wasn't individual therapy for Ellie. Trevor and Ellie needed family therapy to work on the safety of emotional closeness. Trevor also benefited from individual therapy examining and shifting his self-protecting behaviors to more connecting behaviors.

According to Karine Dubois-Comtois and colleagues in the *Journal of Child and Adolescent Behavior*, child psychologist Frédéric Atger has found that "parents often feel distressed and powerless in coping with their adolescent's difficulties, which activates their own attachment system, potentially contributing to the development of an insecure attachment relationship with their adolescent."[2]

Reflecting on your own attachment style (how you were raised and how you tend to act now) will help you create a more secure attachment with your own child.

Reflecting on Parenting Approaches: Avoid Parenting by Default

The construct or philosophy you follow in raising your children is your parenting approach (sometimes called parenting style).[3] The parenting approach used greatly impacts the relationship between parent and teen, and this variable factors into parent-teen attachment.[4] One's parenting approach often echoes that of one's parents. Your historical experiences drive your interactions and often inform how you guide your children.

Today's social scientists recognize five approaches to parenting. Four basic approaches to parenting have long been defined as *authoritarian, authoritative, permissive*, and *neglectful*. Recently, you may have heard about the fifth approach, *overinvolved* (also known as the helicopter, snowplow, or lawnmower parent). As you reflect on your past, think about your own experience growing up. It sometimes helps to look at parenting approaches through the lens of a child.

Authoritative Parenting Approach

Parents who take an authoritative approach nurture, support, and respond to their children, yet they set firm limits and boundaries as needed, with kindness, compassion, and authority. Children of authoritative parents may feel like this: "My parents were nurturing and felt close. They set realistic boundaries, goals, and expectations. Communication and respect were bidirectional. When I misbehaved, it was a conversation with consequences, not just about being punished. I was able to express myself emotionally and felt their warmth and support."

Authoritarian Parenting Approach

Authoritarian parenting is the "command and control" approach. Children of authoritarian parents may feel like this: "My parents' interaction with me was largely focused on controlling and restricting my behavior. I was expected to obey, and my mistakes were punished. Communication and respect went one way, parent to teen. My parents were not emotional, other than showing anger. They offered little or no emotional support to me."

Jill's Story: Authoritative Mom Working to Break Authoritarian Patterns

"I am really struggling right now. Our house feels chaotic, and I can't get a handle on my own emotions. I seem to get triggered easily and fly off the handle at my kids. I don't want to ruin my relationship with them, but it seems to be heading in that direction," confided Jill, a forty-five-year-old mom of a fourteen-year-old daughter and sixteen-year-old son.

As her kids were getting older and given more freedom, she felt increasingly anxious. Even though her kids followed the rules for the most part, she had this unexplainable sense that someone was going to get in trouble. She said, "When they ask me about the rules or push back, I blow up! I almost feel rageful. I hate it."

After working with Jill, we discovered rulemaking was a big trigger for her emotional escalation. Growing up, her father would never allow any questioning of the rules. If he felt even the slightest pushback, he would either yell or threaten to hit her.

When we get emotionally triggered, we may start to parent our kids the same way we were parented, even though we don't want to.

Permissive Parenting Approach

Permissive parenting is warm but undisciplined. Children of permissive parents may feel like this: "My parents were warm and nurturing. There was open communication. However, they seemed more like my friend than a parent. There was a lack of boundaries, control, and inconsistency. They had few (or no) expectations of me. They seemed unconcerned about my growth and maturity. There were no consequences to my sometimes mischievous behavior. I had to figure out a lot on my own."

Beth's Story: Learning from Two Parents with Differing Parenting Approaches (Authoritarian and Permissive—a Common Scenario)

Thirty-year-old Beth described growing up as being "hard." Her father's military career meant her family uprooted every two years, requiring her to make new friends each time. Growing up, Beth felt she could never be totally settled. Even tougher, her parents had conflicting ideals. Her father's parenting style was authoritarian, while her mother's was permissive. This resulted in conflict and turmoil at home.

Beth's strict father related to her devoid of feelings, apart from anger. Beth didn't feel she had a voice. He shut her down quickly when she tried to share feelings or opinions. Her dad monopolized the discussion, lecturing or yelling about the slightest misstep. He would blame her for his anger, saying hurtful things about her character. The relationship was largely about him demanding her respect. It was intensely stressful and often scary.

Most of the time, Beth tried her best to be perfect. She figured if she did everything right, she could avoid getting in trouble. Yet as a teen, she began getting angry at his aggressive nature. She grew tired of feeling scared in her own home. She started challenging her father, which as you can imagine resulted in family explosions.

Beth's mother was warm and loving yet not a completely safe space for her either. Beth said, "She felt more like a friend than a parent. My mother hated conflict, and I think she feared my father too." Her mother often didn't intervene when her father got aggressive. Sometimes when she tried to get involved, it created a bigger, even more stressful fight. Her mom continually tried her best to mitigate conflict, attempting to please everyone at home. When Beth's dad was absent, her mom was inconsistent. She seemed to have a hard time deciding whether Beth and her brother should follow the rules or not. Mom would blame herself for the family discord but say there was nothing she could do. Beth knew her mother was trying but felt her mother didn't care enough to stand up to her father and protect her.

Beth's focus on what to do (or not do) to avoid getting in trouble left her constantly anxious. As an adult, she had trouble making decisions. Beth grew quite unsure of herself, resulting in low self-esteem. She would vacillate from creating a highly structured life of accomplishments to living with virtually no structure, accomplishing little. She felt bad in either scenario, struggling with anxiety and depression. Even as she tried to avoid aggressive personalities like her father's, she continually fell into relationships that felt similar.

Beth's story is an example of growing up with two different parenting styles. One that felt controlling (authoritarian) and another that felt too lax and inconsistent (permissive).

Neglectful Parenting Approach

Neglectful parents are relatively unresponsive to their kids. Children of neglectful parents may feel like this: "My parents took care of my basic needs but were uninvolved, detached, and offered little nurturing. They seemed disinterested in my life. I had a lot of freedom but felt like I was on my own."

Mia's Story: Teens Still Need Their Parents to Be Present

Mia shared with me, "Since I turned thirteen, my parents have gradually become more absent in my life. They claim since I can legally stay at home by myself, they can get their life back. In the last year, it has gotten to the point where they travel for a week at a time, leaving me home by myself."

She continued, "I know most seventeen-year-olds might think this is great, but it just doesn't feel good to me. It feels like I don't have any stability. There are no rules, expectations, or guidance. They seem focused on their own lives, and I don't feel like I am a priority to them any longer."

Overinvolved Parenting Approach

Overinvolved parents often step in, trying to protect their children from setbacks. Children of overinvolved parents may feel like this: "My parents were nurturing but intensely involved in all parts of my life. They felt intrusive and unnecessarily over-protective and controlling. I felt like they didn't think I was capable."

Kalie's Story: Overinvolved Parenting

When Kalie was a junior in high school, she and her mother came to my office together, searching for a way to deal with escalating conflict. Their interactions were mainly about school and getting into a good college. Kalie's mother would constantly check her grades even though Kalie had straight As. Their relationship had reached a point where Kalie was short with her mother, lashing out in anger when discussing anything.

After a few sessions, Kalie shared, "I wish you just believed in me. Why don't you trust that I know what I am doing?" Kalie's mother was shocked. She didn't realize that Kalie was seeing her involvement with school as sending a message of her being incapable. Kalie also shared her wishes for more time spent enjoying each other rather than just focusing on school.

The Volley Lies in the Authoritative Parenting Approach

As you may have gleaned from the examples above, authoritative parenting has more overall positive effects on emotional development, self-esteem, and relationship success. It is also correlated with fewer delinquency behaviors and is associated with a secure attachment.[5]

Reflecting on your own parenting, you may have varying approaches in certain areas or with certain children. Are you authoritative in most situations, except when dealing with a highly reactive teen? Are you concerned you are sometimes neglectful or sometimes overinvolved? That's natural. Most likely your attachment style and parenting approach each correspond with those of one or both of your parents. Your teen has the potential to follow suit—as well as future generations. However, you have influence.

Look at your parenting and be curious about the level of control you seek to establish with your teen. Are you allowing your teen to build autonomy? Teens need structure and boundaries but a healthy balance of independence as well.

If you use the word *control* to talk about parenting your teen, you might be relying on it too much. Controlling parents may seek to dominate teens' behavior, psychology, or both. When the parent-child relationship seeks to control a child through means of guilt, shame, or withdrawal of love (psychological control), it can have detrimental effects on a teen's emotional well-being. Dysfunctional attitudes can lead to vulnerability to anxiety and depression. Using psychological control is never a good parenting tactic.

Self-esteem is a major factor contributing to adolescents' mental health. A study by the Department of Child and Adolescent Psychiatry demonstrated that "adolescents with high self-esteem suffer fewer symptoms of anxiety/depression and attention problems over time, indicating that self-esteem acts as a resilience factor against such symptoms."[6] One could infer that the parenting approach that best supports high self-esteem would be the most beneficial parenting approach for teens. Parents cultivate strong self-esteem through the presence of emotional warmth, loving affection, acceptance, and a balance of autonomy and guidance.

When thinking about parenting approaches and secure attachment, simply ask yourself, "Is my parenting approach compromising a secure attachment?" Looking through the lens of attachment while parenting helps.

Jennifer's Story: Erupting like a Volcano, Feeling Out of Control

Jennifer, a twenty-nine-year-old married, stay-at-home mother, had recently noticed a disconcerting shift. Her first child was three years old, and things had been going well overall, but Jennifer had been noticing a physical sensation arising inside that frightened her.

As she was rushing to get out the door one morning, she asked her son to pick up his toys and put them away. Generally a very pleasant and compliant child, he refused to listen. Jennifer said she felt a "volcano erupting," starting from the pit of her stomach and rising into her chest as her toddler defied her! She felt the need to grab his arm and yell in his face.

This had frightened her. She knew that yelling wasn't something she really wanted to do, but the urge felt so visceral, she almost felt compelled to follow through with the actions.

She sat down and cried. She knew where that reaction came from— her mom. Emotions and memories of her childhood flooded Jennifer.

Jennifer recalled her mother dealing with stress just as she had this day with her son. She could see clearly her mother gritting her teeth, getting close to her and screaming in her face, grabbing her arm. However, she remembered her mother reacted inconsistently.

Jennifer told me, "We got good at knowing when to engage with Mom. If she had a certain look on her face, a kind of scowl, and if she made sounds of being exasperated . . . we knew not to approach her. We didn't have the understanding to know that meant she was stressed; we always thought it was about us, and we knew to get out of her way. To deal with our panic, we would try to do things to please her."

When meeting with parents for the first time, whether about their teen or during couples' work, the question "What was it like for you growing up?" generally brings up a lot of stuff. Parents share their difficult histories, times of confusion, loneliness, fear, and even traumatic events in their own home.

Trying to figure out how to move forward in a different way with your own children can be confusing. It can feel like stuck energy or a continual feeling of moving two steps forward and one back.

Old Wounds Resurface When You Become a Parent

When adults start a family, old wounds resurface from their childhood. These old hurts may even have been processed before, but some new reactions surface when you have a child of your own.

While often the happiest of times, days with your young child may also bring feelings of sadness that can be hard to explain. Sadness may bubble up as you experience your new infant's life, feeling closeness and love, wondering how your parents might have treated you a certain way. It can feel like crushing pain to revisit those hurts at this time, in this new way.

The realization of how things may have been can come flooding back. You may continue the cycle from your family of origin unless you gain new awareness and take steps to do things differently.

The Way You Parent Today Relates to How You Were Parented

Some of the past ideas of how to parent were less than giving. As discussed, parenting was largely about children obeying and being seen and not heard, about using fear-based tactics and physical aggression. There can be a lot to unpack when it comes to your family of origin.

Many people old enough to be parents of teenagers today were not asked how they were feeling or what their opinion was when they were growing up. They were told what to do, and if they didn't obey, punishment was delivered.

As a result, children typically feared their parents. Respect only went one way, from teen to parent. After hearing that parents are their child's primary attachment figures, you can imagine what impact that must have on a child to fear the closest person to them.

If this was your scenario, I am truly sorry for your past circumstances. And I wonder what walls you might have created to self-protect in order to survive in this type of environment. Those walls had purpose before, but they no longer serve you in raising your own children.

Reflecting on Past Trauma's Impact on Parenting

While this is not a deep dive into the psychology behind trauma, touching on this large and complex subject is important. Trauma holds the potential to make a huge impact on how you connect with others, including your teen.

Some of the case studies that have been shared are examples of parents' past experiences with trauma—such as abuses, losses, and shocks. In general, trauma is a lasting emotional response to stress and fear. It can be confusing to know what is trauma and what is just an old wound with unpleasant feelings.

Defining Trauma

The APA Dictionary of Psychology defines trauma as "any disturbing experience that results in significant fear, helplessness, dissociation, confusion, or other disruptive feelings intense enough to have a long-lasting negative effect on a person's attitudes, behavior, and other aspects of functioning."[7]

There are three types of trauma: acute, chronic, and complex. Acute trauma is a single event, such as an accident, natural disaster, or assault. Chronic trauma is a traumatic event that repeats, which could be sexual abuse, physical abuse, psychological abuse, bullying, or domestic violence. Complex trauma is exposure to multiple traumatic events.

Self-reflecting on your own trauma history is vital to understanding your own thoughts, feelings, and patterns. Unfortunately, trauma is a common experience. As you'll recall from chapter 2, about 64 percent of US adults report experiencing ACEs before age eighteen. This means many parents have been exposed to trauma, which may affect how they parent. Further, "ACEs are linked to chronic health problems, mental illness, and substance use problems in adolescence and adulthood."[8]

Memories of traumatic events can be somewhat blurred or chopped up—not a cohesive order of events. The memory can be an overall feeling, a sense of what it was like. Trauma negatively impacts your mental health and has even been found to negatively impact your physical health.

As mental health has taken a back seat to physical health, those who are aware of childhood trauma may not have received the needed help to manage the long-term effects. Others may not even realize their experience has had an impact on them.

Generational Trauma Gets Passed Down

Trauma can affect your attachment style, parenting approach, and communication tendencies with your teen. These patterns of engagement impact how you are with your teen, as discussed. They can bring up a negative cycle of interaction.

Ruby and Ian's Story: Childhood Trauma Creating a Cycle of Pain

Jim (age thirty-eight) and Ian (age twelve) came to me for family therapy. Eruptions in their home were becoming a daily occurrence. They both were upset and wished to have a more peaceful relationship as they had when Ian was younger.

Ian described feeling smothered by his father: "He is constantly hovering, and I can never have an independent thought. All our conversations feel like goal-oriented discussions, and I am overscheduled."

Ian's father responded, "I am just trying to be a good parent. I want to give you as many opportunities as I can. Opportunities that I was not given." Ian quickly chimed in, "It doesn't have to be in every moment of the day."

Jim was confused that Ian saw his involvement as smothering and overbearing. He commented, "I'm just doing what good parents do." I asked Jim about his experience with his own parents. He described feelings of loneliness. He felt like he was mostly on his own. Jim recalled at one point telling himself, "It's all up to me. I can't count on my parents for anything but the roof over my head."

Jim described little guidance and even minimal interaction with his parents. He felt he had to be self-sufficient and figure it all out on his own after about fourth grade. Jim's parents' neglect was traumatic and undoubtedly caused him anxiety. This trauma resulted in him being overinvolved with Ian in an effort to give him the attention and guidance he didn't receive from his own parents. Jim's childhood trauma played a part in the negative cycle of interaction with Ian. His overinvolvement caused conflict and disconnection in his relationship with Ian.

You can become activated during stressful situations with your teen, leading you to parent in a way you normally would not choose. Becoming emotionally triggered can result in less than pleasing feelings and activation of your central nervous system. When your system is activated, you go into a distress reaction. You may become anxious. Needing to calm your anxiety, you may overshelter your teen. Not allowing them to take healthy risks in an effort to keep them safe is a sign of trauma. You may also become angry and react in rash ways. Alternately, emotional triggers may cause you to shut down or try to escape, all of which cause disconnection and can influence a parent's ability to attend to their teen's emotional needs. All of these scenarios create distance between you and your teen.

Generational trauma (also called transgenerational trauma, intergenerational trauma, or ancestral trauma) is trauma(s) experienced by a parent and passed off to their offspring. The traumatic events could be a direct personal experience like physical abuse or sexual abuse, being witness to events such as domestic violence or discrimination, or a collective exposure to events like war, terrorist attacks, or shootings. These unresolved traumatic experiences can be passed down from one generation to the next. This kind of trauma can be transferred through behavior, attitudes (from parents' modeling and interactions), and even DNA.

Trauma may be passed through psychological transference of the events (as when a family member recalls a traumatic event through storytelling). A parent's stress response can be passed down without the child actually experiencing the traumatic event: Rachel Yehuda and Amy Lehrner, pioneers in the study of epigenetics, have noted, "A more recent and provocative claim is that the experience of trauma—or more accurately the effect of that experience—is 'passed' somehow from one generation to the next through non-genomic, possibly epigenetic mechanisms affecting DNA function or gene transcription."[9]

Generational trauma can lead to mental health issues such as post-traumatic stress disorder (PTSD), anxiety, or depression.

Parents' fears become their kids' fears. Stress lingers even when a threat is no longer present. As Bruce Perry, MD, PhD, has written in his book, *What Happened to You?*, coauthored with Oprah, "Humans are emotionally 'contagious'; we sense the distress of others. . . . The parent's internal storm becomes the home's storm."[10]

Theo's Story: Carrying Generational Trauma

Theo's mind frequently told him, "I must have done something, and they must be mad at me."

Theo, a twenty-year-old sophomore in college, was referred to me by his parents for help with his high anxiety. Theo had difficulty with continual thoughts that someone was mad or that he was not liked by his peers. Social media only complicates these issues. Seeing others' locations, delayed responses in texting, or texts being left unread would cause a spiral of negative thoughts.

In one session, Theo was worried his father, Jon, was upset with him. Jon checked in with Theo by text morning and night. If Theo didn't respond, Jon would then call. If Theo didn't answer the call, his father would text again, asking, "Are you okay?" "Is everything all right?" or even "Are you alive?"

Jon always needed to know if Theo was okay. The inquiries would quickly escalate, with Jon thinking a catastrophic event occurred if Theo didn't answer. Jon always seemed to fear the worst, regularly mentioning precautions Theo should be taking. Jon would always make a few safety comments (with a tone that sounded more angry than concerned) before hanging up, saying, "Make sure you have gas," or "Make sure no one puts drugs in your drink."

Theo often felt his father was angry with him. He wasn't sure why. Nothing catastrophic had ever happened. Yet he felt he was continually looking for the most horrific thing to happen—just like his father.

I soon discovered that Jon's sister had unexpectedly died when he was four years old. Jon's parents (Theo's grandparents) suppressed their grief, never seeking help. They became oversheltering, keeping close tabs on Jon, continually trying to anticipate or mitigate disaster—when there was no disaster in sight. Their high anxiety was always present. Theo was carrying that same anxiety around with him every day, yet he was unaware of it. The cycle continued.

Your experience is impacted by your parents' experience. Their experience was impacted by their parents' experience and so on and so on. Look at your history and notice how trauma may be affecting your parenting. This could be childhood trauma or even a traumatic event that occurred outside your family home.

Reflecting on Identity: Culture, Religion, Geography, Socioeconomic Status, and Generational Cues

Each person's core identity is shaped—beyond the huge influence their parents and their first family have on them—by culture, religion, geography, socioeconomic status, and generational messages. Culture pervades every aspect of parenting, starting even before inception. Parents start planning how they want to raise their child, how they will interact with their child, what behaviors they deem as ideal, and what they want to expose their child to. Culture, religion, geographic location, socioeconomic status, and the generation you were born into directly impact those choices.

Children absorb such influences, developing how they think and view themselves according to specific customs and beliefs. Various pressures exist and opportunities arise depending on where someone lives, their culture, and socioeconomic status. These factors influence how you develop, affecting your emotional, physical, and linguistic states as well as your social tendencies.

Culture even influences parenting before the child is born. In a peer-reviewed article on cultural approaches to parenting, Marc H. Bornstein noted, "Culture-specific influences on development and parenting begin long before children are born, and they shape fundamental decisions about which behaviors parents should promote in their children and how parents should interact with their children."[11]

Culture Influences Us, Whether We Know It or Not

Parent-teen relationships, parenting approaches, and even parental warmth are greatly influenced by culture. Individuals tend to think of culture as something outside themselves, but cultural influences shape everything a person does, often flying "below the radar" of consciousness. Therapists most frequently see culture showing up in expectations, standards, and values.

Culture impacts the view of self, communication tendencies, accepted behaviors, role expectations (including children's roles), value placed on the needs of the individual versus the whole, and how relationships function. Culture says how much time to spend practicing traditions and cultivating a sense of belonging. Culture impacts our core beliefs and value systems. Culture influences physical development, social and emotional development, and cognitive development.

Culture influences how you cope with stress, how you relate to adversity, whether you recognize mental disorders, and even your willingness to seek help when mental health problems arise. Stigma or discrimination can also influence the diagnosis and treatment of mental health problems in a culture.

Reflecting on My Own Cultural Influences

When I think about the influence of culture, I think about my Italian grandmother, Philomena—how warm and caring she was. Philomena made it evident that life was indeed about family—cooking together and taking time at the table for conversation. In Italy, entire families can be seen strolling together after sharing a long meal, taking a nightly *passeggiata*. Italians stereotypically pamper babies and enjoy big families. And Italians are famously emotive! My grandmother absolutely prioritized family time and gave me deep feelings of connectedness when we spent time together. I felt that emotional closeness even when we were physically apart. Thinking of her and our relationship would bring me comfort and calm in times of distress.

While I don't profess to be an expert on any culture or subculture, I've seen how deeply unseen cultural forces influence groups of people. When living on the East Coast, Midwest, and the southern United States, I saw major differences in how people relate to one another. From what subjects they discussed to how they conversed, each region was distinct. I've also worked with people of many international backgrounds as part of my work as a therapist. Cultural influences can be easily seen with couples of differing backgrounds. It is evident how religion, geographic location, and ethnicity affect how couples communicate. The words a person uses to communicate reflect culture and geographic location. Linguistic nuances impact the exchange between two people. Even the way people express and experience emotions can vary from culture to culture.

In my opinion, parents benefit greatly by reflecting on their own cultural upbringing—looking at it objectively, as a social scientist would. The more we are aware of culture, the better able we are to make conscious choices about how we want to be. Cultural influences can, to a degree, help or hinder emotional connections between parents and teens.

Culture tells us about family. Culture shapes the development of beliefs and values in both the entire family and each individual within it. It tells you what family means and how a family functions. It defines gender norms, including the treatment of gender roles. Defines what it means to be successful. How much time is spent with immediate family, extended family, and working. It even dictates how children address adults, such as "sir" and "ma'am."

Various cultures treat the teenage years differently, viewing the time of adolescence in different ways. Some acknowledge adolescence with a public ceremony, while other cultures view this time as a hurdle to overcome or even a problem to get through.

Culture may be collectivist or individualist. Societies tell members how to value the needs of everyone in the group (needs as a whole versus individual needs). This impacts autonomy during adolescent years. Western cultures tend to value independence. In collectivist societies, connectedness of the whole is valued. There are different social norms and expectations around these values. Dating and career choices are two examples where family influence matters more in collectivist culture. Culture even tells us what positions of authority and level of obedience to expect.

Religion Shapes Identity, Morality, and Self-Talk

Religion provides a framework for moral decision-making. What a person learns about religion as a child often continues to govern their behavior over the long term. Religion may guide how you see yourself and how you talk to yourself.

Globally, there is a trend toward living without formal religion or being agnostic or atheist, and that shapes a teen's worldview as well. Whether or not they follow a formal religion, parents teach their children a set of morals, ethics, principles, and values based on how they live and model certain behaviors around their kids.

Religion shapes identity too. As one example, if a teenager is gay and the religion is not accepting of those who are gay, the individual may start to feel shame and guilt about who they are. They may have to disown or hide parts of themselves. As another example, religion might shape a person's identity as "a giver" or "a contributor" to a community greater than oneself.

Religion can help create many community connections, which may help individuals feel less isolated. However, a person can belong to a religious community and still not have a sense of fully belonging. Belonging requires being seen for who you truly are.

Geographic Location Shapes Your Identity

Where you are raised also impacts who you are and how you develop. Geographic areas influence the general lifestyle of inhabitants. Even down to the clothes worn, geographic areas have influence. Certain geographic locations emphasize the importance of making connections within a community, while others do not.

Environmental factors mold a person, impacting their worldview and how they fit into this large world. It influences their thoughts about themselves and who others are, including how they build connections with others, how they interact with anyone outside of their family of origin, and how they cope. Is there a feeling of safety or not?

Mental health varies by rural, urban, and other factors.[12] Surroundings have been shown to impact mood and mental health, plus access to health services. Location also determines whether treatments and legal or illegal substances are readily available.

Socioeconomic Factors Affect Status and Much More

Socioeconomic factors typically include income, education, and employment, and they may also include community safety and access to social support. Socioeconomics shapes a person's worldview, such as how one sees abundance, scarcity, growth, and career opportunities. Perceptions about a person's socioeconomic "standing" (yours and others) may impact feelings about them and behavior around them—wittingly or unwittingly.

Your financial status impacts the opportunities available to you (academic, economic, career). It speaks to where you live (affluent or impoverished, urban or rural, peaceful or violent). It influences your sense of community and much more.

It is important to mention that socioeconomic factors can both create and maintain race and ethnic disparities. Social and economic status determines a person's access to physical and mental health care. Overall, health can impact family life and economic well-being too.

As you reflect on your past, consider how your socioeconomic status may have affected you over time or may be affecting you now. In capitalist societies, the status can change often—even wealthy families and individuals experience windfalls and lean times. Other families or individuals may be caught in a cycle of perpetual struggle. Consider how socioeconomic factors affect your mental health, your ability to seek treatment, and how you relate to others.

Generational Messages Influence Thoughts and Perceptions

Generational messages influence who you are. The times you live in affect what messages you hear growing up—at times when our core identity is shaped. As you grow up, political leadership, states of war/peace, industry, economic climate, technology, and media and pop culture all influence how you think.[13] Generational messaging influences what we deem important, what we feel comfortable talking about, and how we relate to others. Messaging impacts our home and professional lives and the balance between the two.

The following are the different generational cohorts:

The Greatest Generation: Born 1901 to 1924, grew up during the Great Depression. They fought in World War II.

The Silent Generation: Born 1925 to 1945, grew up post–World War II. They may have fought in the Korean War or the Vietnam War.

Baby Boomers (a.k.a. Boomers): Born 1946 to 1964. Influenced by the Vietnam War and/or counterculture.

Generation X (Gen X): Born 1965 to 1980. Known as "latchkey kids" due to growing dual-income families, the need for children to be self-reliant. The "MTV generation."

Millennials (Gen Y): Born from 1981 to 1996. Digital natives. Impacted by 9/11.

Generation Z (Gen Z): Born 1997 to 2012. First iPhone. Climate worries, COVID-19 pandemic.

Generation Alpha (or Gen Alpha): Born from 2013 to mid-2025. Fully immersed in the digital world (born after smartphones and the iPad were introduced).

Take a moment to reflect on your generation and what lessons you learned growing up. What generational messages do you notice your teenager absorbing today? You may not think this would be the case, but your worldview and opinions might be different today if you had been born in a different era. Things have changed dramatically since you were a teenager. Think about the speed of technology, the access to news and media, and other factors influencing your teen today.

Generation Alpha, teens now, are exposed to more technology at a younger age than any other generation. They are more aware of mental health concepts and terminology. They have immediate access to a global view of news, information, and influencers. They are taking in an abundance of messaging daily from various sources and many with little parental supervision. Specifically, teens spend an average of 4.8 hours per day on social media, according to a Gallup article.[14] That means exposure to a wide range of information and messaging. In the past, parents were more likely to watch shows with their kids and chime in to add context, assuage fears, and share thoughts about values. Today, many kids are left to sift through an onslaught of information themselves.

Generational Differences When It Comes to Talking Mental Health

"I was diagnosed with bipolar disorder a year ago. I went into treatment after having my first manic episode at nineteen. I was drinking alcohol excessively, not sleeping, and making risky decisions," Randall shared in our first session.

I asked Randall if bipolar disorder or any other mental health issues ran in his family. He said, "Yes, my mother told me that my father has bipolar disorder. She also said that she has anxiety."

I asked, "You said your mother mentioned your father has bipolar disorder. Has he spoken with you about his experience and how he manages his illness?"

Randall said, "No, he won't talk to me about it. I've gotten in trouble for actions related to my illness—excessive drinking, spending money—but he doesn't talk to me about my bipolar. I don't get it. It makes me feel worse."

Even though Randall's father has the same illness as Randall, his refusal to speak openly to his son is a direct result of generational messaging.

Generational messages influence not only how we think but also what we talk about, how we view ourselves and others, and (possibly) how we pass judgment on both. One consistent message over generations has been "We don't talk about our mental health with others, even our own children and families."

The stigma around mental health has been a long-standing issue. According to the APA, Gen Z discusses mental health more openly than any other generation.[15] Gen Z and now Generation Alpha have found a wealth of information online, gaining knowledge about mental health in just a few clicks. These generations see others—including influencers—sharing openly about their mental health, normalizing the conversation.

Again, we see a widening generational gap between parents and teens regarding conversations about mental health. Tweens, teens, and young adults may try to initiate conversations and share about their own mental health with their parents, who grew up with the subject being taboo. The generational gap also includes discussion of feelings because you can't talk about mental health without talking about your feelings.

Takeaway: View Your Relationships through Attachment Patterns and Learn to Sustain the Volley

If you approach your relationship with your teen from an attachment lens, you can see clearer. This is true of any relationship.

Using an attachment lens, you can identify how your communication tendencies (from chapter 3) and parenting approaches can promote or interrupt cultivating a secure attachment. Having looked to the past, you may now recognize patterns in your action tendencies, behaviors, underlying themes, and associated feelings.

Please know that people don't always interact from the same attachment style in each of their relationships. You can shift between them depending on what is going on around you, who you are interacting with, and your current state of mind and mood.

Even if secure attachment has not been established by adolescence, it can still be developed. However, it may require additional support from a mental health professional. Parents may need support in making shifts, especially if a secure attachment is not something they had themselves with their parents growing up. Please see the list of national mental health resources on page 217.

The next chapter helps you further reflect on your internal experience in your present-day interactions. With self-reflection practices, you can distill what's happening during your current volleys and sustain a healthy back-and-forth volley with your teens. Keeping attachment front and center ensures connectedness as the goal.

Chapter 4 Reflection: Styles and Past Experiences

After reading about the various attachment styles, parenting approaches, and communication tendencies (from chapter 3), think about these questions:

- What are my styles?
  - Where do I presently fall in my attachment style?
  - Where do I presently fall in my parenting approach?
  - Is my parenting approach creating secure attachment?
  - Are my communication tendencies (from chapter 3) matching up with a secure attachment model?
- Where does it come from?
  - Am I just following what my experience was growing up?
  - When parenting my teen, what do I want to incorporate from my own childhood experience?

- What intentional changes do I want to make from my own childhood experience in parenting my teen?
- How do I want my child to feel in my presence?
  - What do I want my relationship to look and feel like to my teen?
  - Does my cultural upbringing emphasize secure connection?
  - Do my cultural influences align with how I want to interact with my teen today?
  - Is my culture a source of strength, stress, or both?

CHAPTER 5

Introspection

Tracking the Senses Within

Reviewing your past (as in the last chapter) is important. Hopefully you found reflecting back useful as a way to appreciate what informs your way of being today. However, please know that the goal is not to live in the past. Getting stuck in the past can be painful, and it only hinders your ability to move forward and evolve.

The goal of looking back is to discover what old "stuff" may be showing up in the present. You were looking for anything interfering with your ability to feel connectedness with others, especially your teen today.

When Relating to Your Teen, Self-Reflect in the Moment

After you've taken time to look at your past, another way to help establish a healthy relationship with your teen is to look at what's happening within yourself—now, daily, and in times of stress. Introspection is an essential process in any relationship.

What happens to you daily impacts your children and how they feel in their relationship with you. While in the ever-important role of mom or dad, you are most likely juggling a career and financial responsibilities, preparing healthy meals, participating in household duties, and caring for yourself. These multiple roles no doubt bring stress into your life. How you handle your inner world becomes a model for your children.

When your teen sees your willingness for introspection, they sense their importance to you. When they witness you being intentional in your interactions with them, they feel your care. Your own self-reflection may even feel more important to them than what you do for them.

Do You Spend Time Reflecting on Your Own Emotions and Feelings?

Envisioning a feeling of connectedness with your teen first means embracing your own emotions and feelings. Historically, emotions and feelings may not have been well attended to, cared for, or discussed. What lessons did you receive regarding emotional processing?

Now it's clear that emotions and feelings tell us more about what is happening. Tuning in can be helpful. This doesn't mean you need to examine every single emotion or feeling that arises. It means noticing what might be influencing your mood, functioning, and relationships and taking steps to understand the impact. This enables you to move through difficult emotions, which can prevent you from destructive patterns of ruminating (dwelling on negative thoughts) or suppressing (stuffing down). Processing emotions helps safeguard you from their lingering effects.

To deal with these suppressed emotions, we may use unhealthy means to cope. Alcohol, substances, gambling, and even food can be ways we cope with unprocessed feelings. Often when individuals reach rehab, they talk about buried feelings that led to their use. As noted in the last chapter, when you don't process how you feel, it can leave you not understanding your own needs—ultimately interfering in your day-to-day lives and your relationships.

Further, as previously mentioned, today's teens have been exposed to lessons and information about psychology that are new to the educational or media landscape. Parents weren't exposed to these things growing up. A widening gap exists between parents and teens on these topics. Teens may know more about their own emotions and feelings than their parents. This affects parent-teen interactions.

You Are Always Broadcasting Feelings, and Your Teen Notices

Parents often think they are hiding their feelings well. However, those around you (especially your children) sense more than you know. How you feel—whether calm, stressed, enthusiastic, or anxious at any given moment—seeps into your interactions with others, especially your teen(s).

You may feel justified to stay on autopilot because you are under a tremendous amount of pressure. Or you may be completely unaware you have become numb to emotional sensitivity. It happens.

When adults operate on autopilot (understandable given their daily tasks), they are not allowing themselves to truly be in their own bodies. How could you know your emotional state when you are only thinking rather than sensing?

Processing Body Sensations, Emotions, Thoughts, and Feelings

While you may have learned to prioritize thoughts, the truth is that body sensations, emotions, thoughts, and feelings work together as a comprehensive feedback loop system. You can use all of your senses while taking in an experience. When someone is cooking, you sense your stomach growling, and you may even salivate. You can hear the sizzling, smell the aroma, see the food, and taste the flavors. Each sense impacts your experience of the meal.

When you only tune into your thoughts, ignoring emotions and feelings, it is like you aren't acknowledging all your available senses. Emotions and feelings can impact and enhance thoughts too. They affect your experience with others and help you move to engage. Body sensations, emotions, thoughts, and feelings all matter.

Due to teens' stage of brain development, their felt sense of emotions reverberates loudest. Parents in tune with their own emotional states use feelings to better facilitate connections with teens. Parents who try to rule teens with logic alone fight a futile battle.

Four Steps to "Go Within" and Gain Awareness

When you slow things down and focus on your internal experience, you'll gain useful awareness. Try these four important steps:

Step 1: Notice what body sensations and initial emotions are happening.
Step 2: Notice your action tendencies.

Step 3: Notice what thoughts are occurring.

Step 4: Notice the feelings underneath that are coming up.

By noticing these four things, you can become more in tune with yourself and begin to better understand what's happening between you and your teen (the focus of the next chapter).

Parents who learn to process physical sensations, action tendencies, thoughts, and feelings can teach teens to do the same. You can start with body sensations. Are you able to acknowledge how your body is responding?

In-Depth Case Study: How Christine Went from Yelling (Escalated) to Sensing (De-escalated)

In this chapter, we'll be looking at how my client Christine learned to stop yelling. There were a few steps to her self-reflection process, and we'll go over each step one by one.

Christine first came to me with concerns about her yelling at her eleven-year-old daughter, Grace. She described that it wasn't until a few minutes after she yelled that she realized what was happening. Then a flood of bad feelings, guilt, and disgust would flush over her.

I asked her about her parents' interactions with her growing up. She described always mitigating being in trouble. Anything from not cleaning the dishes well enough to getting a B in school could spark a negative interaction and her being reprimanded.

She and I discussed using her body sensations as a starting point to help reduce the yelling. I gave her an exercise, sensing what was happening in her body the moment she had the urge to yell.

Christine came back the next week discouraged. She said she never felt anything in her body before she yelled.

I reassured Christine that this can be common and that she would get to a point where she could feel her own bodily reactions. It might just take some time. I explained that she most likely had a heightened state of dysregulation at home growing up, and an unconscious shutting down of her body sensations was likely a way she dealt with her home environment.[1] I gave her one more exercise: "In a quiet space, put your headphones on and listen to your favorite song. Notice any physical sensations. Then change the song and notice what happens in your body."

Christine worked hard and learned to tap into her body sensations using what she felt as cues to understand what was going on internally. She learned to sense where she felt discomfort in her body right before she reached the point of yelling. In Christine's case, she felt discomfort in her stomach area, but body sensations show up differently for each person.

Step 1: Notice the Physical Signs within Your Body

Our bodies tell us a lot. If you tune in, your body can lead you in navigating many situations. If you can, envision a barometer. A barometer measures atmospheric pressure. It senses changes in the environment. Your body works in the same way.

For example, what physically happens when sensing someone around you is mad? Does your chest feel tight, your heart rate increase, or your face feel hot? Such physical cues provide a first read on what's happening in the environment. You can key into these sensations and discover times that you get triggered by something or someone. Emotions can be intense but are typically short lived.

When communicating with your teen or really anyone, knowing what your body is telling you is important because it is the first step in getting a handle on the chain of events when communicating. Sometimes it can be the thought you notice first, and then you sense how your body registers. Either way, tuning in will help in your interaction with your teen.

Making it explicit helps. Parents can say something like "My chest is tight right now. I think I need a minute to calm down." By making a commitment to use your body as a barometer, you can help your teen learn to do the same. You'll both improve your ability to stay present and communicate openly and honestly in the moment without getting hijacked by a heightened emotional state.

Step 2: Notice Actions Tied to the Physical Sensations, Thoughts, and Feelings

Action tendencies are tied to emotional states. They represent a desire or an urge to carry out a certain behavior one may or may not execute.

Action Tendency: Attack

When Christine was younger, she often felt trapped at home waiting for something negative to happen. As she reached her teenage years, she would fight back at the slightest conflict with her parents. Looking back now, she realized how anxious she truly was at home.

As an adult, Christine's tendency was to attack when getting into an argument with anyone, including her teenage daughter, Grace.

She started to get better at sensing the urge to attack (yell) because of all the work she had done tuning into her body sensations.

The main action tendencies or stress responses during times of real or perceived threat are to flee (escape by withdrawing or avoiding) or fight (take action or pursue by attacking, approaching, or poking). A third is freeze (becoming immobile).

- You may feel worried or anxious and want to flee.
- You may sense something is hard or uncomfortable (even closeness with someone) and want to avoid and withdraw.

- You may sense you or someone close to you is in danger and feel the urge to fight.
- You may sense something positive and move toward it or want someone's attention and nag.
- You may freeze as you become aware of and process the situation or become temporarily immobile and flop.

A fourth action tendency has been discussed in recent years, fawn. This is when you try to please in the face of a threat.

Again, slow down. Check in to discover what your go-to action tendency might be in various situations.

Step 3: Notice Thoughts Within (Stemming from View of Self)

Have you ever become flooded with thoughts during a high-stakes conversation?

It can be hard to be present during an exchange with your teen as you juggle what is happening internally while trying to figure out what is going on with your teen. Slowing things down and listening to what messages you are telling yourself can be so helpful. Become an observer of the interaction while also participating in the discussion.

When faced with any high-conflict situation, you can go through a quick body scan and process of an appraisal. Look for clues to what's happening internally and how that might be clouding the conversation.

The "inner monologue" going on inside your head when communicating with others stems from your *view of self*. Everyone, including parents, holds beliefs about who they are from messages received throughout life. This shapes how you see yourself (and to some degree, how others see you, too). A subconscious conversation is always running in your mind. You may or may not be aware that it's going on, but it certainly influences and often interferes with communication. Research says that 80 percent of what people say to themselves is negative and 95 percent of what people say to themselves repeats.[2]

Hearing the Inner Critic

One week, I gave Christine an exercise to find out what she was saying to herself all day. I asked her to tune into her thoughts and jot them down in the notes section of her phone over the next week. I didn't want her to feel like she had to do it every day but suggested she jot notes a couple of times during the week—especially on days she seemed to struggle.

Christine came back the next week and sat down on the couch. Her eyes immediately filled up as she said to me, "I say a lot of cruel stuff to myself every day."

She shared much of what she had discovered over the week. Specific to parenting, she was telling herself, "I suck at this. I don't know what I am doing. I am going to mess Grace up. I have no business raising another person. I can't keep it together."

No wonder Christine had been yelling! She was telling herself she couldn't cut it as a parent during her most stressful moments. This only increased her anxiety levels and blocked her ability to effectively deal with the situation at hand.

View of Self: How Background Questions Constantly Run the Mind

The *view of self* includes at least two big questions that everyone runs subconsciously:

- "Who am I?"
- "What do others think and feel about me?"

Internal self-questioning can pose a significant barrier to effective communication. We often "hear" things that actually aren't said. This can lead to assumptions, misunderstandings, and disconnections between parents and teens.

The question "Who am I?" creates beliefs that become part of the interactions and conversations we have with others. The question "What do others think and feel about me?" leads us to carry assumptions about how someone else views us. This is especially the case when it's someone you think you know well—like your parents or kids. The unspoken assumptions about how you feel you're likely to be perceived shade what you say and what you hear.

Most of the time these assumptions go unverified. This causes a lot of confusion. You can take one comment or look, create your own meaning, then wrap your thoughts and feelings around your hypothesis and run with it. It's not always a conscious process either.

The frequency of these background conversations happening in one's head is high. It's a mixture of conversation plus assumptions. This is true for both parents and teens. I often feel like an interpreter in my sessions with the parents and teens. I'll ask, "What did you hear your teen/mom/dad say?"

The responses are filled with a mixture of what the speaker has said and beliefs long carried by the listener. Each person carries assumptions of how others view them, and these can become self-fulfilling prophecies.

The Inner Conversation: Confirming Your Existing Beliefs

I'll share my own inner conversation that originates from my family of origin and still comes up often in my communication with others. It's one where I feel I'm to blame.

If I am communicating with my husband and I historically hold the belief that I am always portrayed as the "bad guy," I filter what the other person is saying through the lens of me being the one at fault.

When I am listening, I am on the hunt for messaging that leads to this belief. It taints the conversation and leads to hearing things that actually aren't said. And my behavior reflects this belief of self.

You have consciously or unconsciously learned what to expect from others in a relationship. To a degree, you get what you expect. You learn certain expectations from your family of origin and your history with other relationships. That comes through in every interaction going forward. You are setting the expectations right now for your teen of what they will expect in relationships with others.

Watch for These Common Cognitive Distortions

Certain patterns of thinking can cause you to view a situation, others, and even yourself inaccurately. Cognitive distortions can cause you to feel bad about yourself, getting in the way of communicating with others, including your teen. Common thought distortions include polarizing, catastrophizing, personalizing, and mind reading.

When you see things as good/bad, black/white, or all/nothing, you miss everything in between; you are *polarizing*. This type of thinking can lead you to being hard on yourself and others. Judgment and rigidness are characteristics of polarizing patterns. This can create narrow thinking and instigate self-judgment and conflict with others. You can end up giving little grace and may quickly end up in a place where you feel the need to be perfect and demand the same of others.

Parenting naturally brings some worries, but parents can get caught thinking about how to mitigate the worst possible scenarios. This is known as *catastrophizing*. Parents may take one mistake (of their own or their teens) and blow it up to a horrific outcome. This may sound like "I forgot to remind my teen about their homework assignment—I am a bad parent!" or "My teen got a C on their test! They won't get into college, and their future is bleak." Comments from teens indicate they may be aware of this problem before parents can see it. They may say, "My mom always thinks of the worst-case scenario."

Because of negativity bias, humans tend to filter life events through a negative lens, but when you blame yourself for everything, you are *personalizing*. Parents often take on their kids' faults or mistakes as their own. They might think, "My teen flunked their geometry test; it's all my fault because I am not good at geometry."

Everyone has a tendency at one time or another to assume they know what others are thinking and feeling, but no one is capable of actually *mind reading*. Parents know their kids well, but that doesn't mean you know what they are thinking and feeling all the time. Mind reading can be a way you get tripped up in communicating with anyone. It sends you down a rabbit hole by making assumptions and jumping to conclusions (usually negative ones) with minimal information.

You can distort your thinking in many more ways, causing you to beat yourself up or create miscommunication. Everyone has automatic thoughts that can be hard to control. Yet you can influence your state of mind by looking at how you take in negative thoughts, what weight you give them, and how you respond. Heightened awareness helps, as does learning what triggers critical thoughts in the first place.

Step 4: Notice the Feelings Within

While your emotions *start* as sensations in the body, additional feelings are generated from your thoughts about those emotions. Being able to name what feelings you are having when communicating is important. Unfortunately, many parents today didn't grow up talking about emotions and feelings. Clients in session (of any age) who are asked how they are feeling often answer that they simply don't know.

Moving the emotional muscle takes practice. You may not realize that you struggle to identify feelings when they arise. If you have never moved a certain muscle in your body, you may not have awareness of that muscle. When finally moving the muscle, it can feel hard to do, awkward, and uncomfortable. You may do it once and never want to do it again due to the discomfort.

What's underneath the Frustration?

Christine knew that she was frustrated when she yelled. That seemed obvious to her. As we talked further, she discovered there was more underneath the frustration.

She was feeling a bit lost and feared that she didn't know how to parent Grace. She was trying desperately to give Grace a different childhood than her own. Up until now life was easy, but there seemed to be a big shift in Grace since turning eleven. Christine also realized that she felt alone parenting all by herself; she was a single mom.

Christine continued to work outside of therapy to be more in tune with how she was feeling. During breaks at work, she would sit quietly for a few minutes and reflect on how she was feeling. She would even jot down a few sentences in those moments.

It's especially helpful to be able to express your feelings clearly when communicating with your teen. Especially when you disagree or are disciplining. Pause and give time to identify what you are feeling. Share, for example, "I am feeling a little overwhelmed. I think I need a few minutes to breathe." Simply stating "I'm angry; I need to calm myself down before we talk" goes a long way.

Your teen will appreciate that you are taking the time to notice your own internal experience. It shows them that you are present in the moment and want to be conscious of how you're feeling and how that may be impacting the exchange of communication.

Anger Often Masks Other Emotions

Anger is often misunderstood. It can be a default expression, a go-to emotion, or a way of defending yourself. Yet anger can be a secondary emotion. It can often be a response to another emotion, like sadness. There can be so much underneath the feeling of anger.

Common emotions that trigger anger include fear, sadness, anxiety, stress, shame, hurt, uncertainty, embarrassment, grief, frustration, and apprehension. These other emotions might cause a person to feel too vulnerable if expressed, so it's common to rely on anger instead.

You need to dig a bit to find out all that is hidden underneath. For example, below anger, you may find "I am feeling embarrassed because I didn't understand what you truly needed" or "I was unsure of how to handle the situation, so I got anxious, and it came across as anger."

What's underneath the Anger?

When Christine expressed frustration, I suggested, "Stop and ask yourself, What is the actual need or want underneath me being critical?"

Often one person becomes critical of another when there is an unexpressed need. Often parents and teens either don't know how to share a feeling or don't feel comfortable expressing their underlying emotional needs.

For example, when you say to your child, "You are always on your phone, get off!" the underlying thought or feeling might be

- "I would like to have some time with you."
- "I need some attention from you."
- "I am bored and want someone to hang out with."
- "I am feeling like a bad parent right now, since you have been on your phone for two hours."
- "I don't know what to do right now; this is uncharted territory for me."

An unexpressed need could be a longing for the other person to do something or a longing to feel a certain way.

When you lead with the feelings *underneath* the anger, your feelings are usually better received. This is because more subtle or complex emotions trigger not fear or defensiveness in the other person but rather empathy. It's hard to be mad at someone who is sharing their sadness, loneliness, or hurt.

Anger's purpose is to let others know you are not content with what is going on—either what's happening internally for you or pertaining to the situation at hand. Something is uncomfortable and you want change, so anger serves to make movement.

It can take a long time to get comfortable with anger when you feel it or when someone else expresses it.

When considering all that is happening within, ask yourself if this is a good time to be communicating with your teen. Ask, "Am I in the right space to communicate, to listen?" It is okay if you aren't, but you need to let your teen know. Tell them it isn't about them; it is about you not feeling you are in a space to hear well.

Developing New Parenting Instincts

As Christine reflected on her parenting, she began to ask herself questions like the following:

Do I want to go with my urge to fight . . . or do I want to stay, be curious, and learn what's happening to my daughter?

Do I want to yell . . . or take a breath and be calm with Grace?

Do I want to tell myself I am a horrible parent . . . or give myself compassion?

Do I want to hide how I am feeling right now . . . or share it?

Christine tried these new approaches to parenting day to day, and her "gut reactions" began to change. I asked Christine to continue to lean in, acknowledging her body reactions, action tendencies, thoughts, and feelings.

As one last exercise, I encouraged Christine to pause and discern, "What is my instinct telling me to do at this moment? Is this an old reflexive instinct or a new chosen one?"

Christine had already learned how her family of origin had impacted her present relationship with Grace. Now she was making incredible progress, seeing positive results in her relationships. She felt trust was being built. Closeness was growing.

Consider the Impact of Mood

Your mood or overall state of mind serves as a major factor in what's going on "within."

Many things can impact your mood and cause fluctuation daily: whether you've gotten a good night's sleep, eaten well, received good or disappointing news, or had bad interactions with others. Someone cutting you off while driving, for example, can quickly shift your mood.

Maybe you are on cloud nine and nothing will bother you. Or you had a difficult day and you feel like you are walking through mud. Emotions and feelings can impact your mood, and your mood can impact your thoughts, feelings, and behavior. State of mind is like an infinity loop in this regard, yet there is more to it. What has happened to you throughout the day isn't the only thing that affects your mood.

Genetics (family history) and biology (a person's specific genes or brain chemistry) play a major role in your mood. To make it more complicated, your life experiences impact how your genes are expressed.

To take it one step further, your mood is a big indicator of your mental health. Moods fluctuate daily, but it is important to consider if there are any patterns occurring. Notice if you tend to feel more down, up, irritable, or nervous. Observe whether your moods fluctuate rapidly or if they linger so that nothing seems to help them shift. Mood affects how you feel internally and how you interact and connect with your teens.

The Kitchen Sink Story: Kids Take on More Than Is Theirs to Own

Kids are egocentric, meaning they feel everything happening must be related to them. This doesn't mean they are selfish; it's just where they are in their development. So they end up taking on more "stuff" than is theirs to own—including parents' moods and nuances of their mental health.

Anxiety is something I personally have struggled with all my life. It comes and goes with or without reason. Some days I am good at keeping it at bay, and other days, when it is running, I show up very differently. One afternoon, I was standing at the sink in our kitchen. I was feeling a bit anxious and overwhelmed with the many tasks on my plate. I recall going through a list of things I needed to accomplish in my head.

My son, who was ten at the time, came over to me and said, "Mom, are you mad at me?" I was taken aback by his question and said, "No, why would you think I was mad at you?" He said I looked mad, and he assumed it was something about him. He had thought to himself, "Have I done anything Mom would be mad about?" He said he was getting worried, thinking he was going to get in trouble.

I shared with him that in no way was I mad at him; he had done nothing wrong. I explained my mental list making and that I guess when I am anxious, I look angry! I told him I was so glad he asked me. I also said, "A hug would be wonderful right now."

From that day on, when my son would see that look on my face, he knew it was only my anxiety taking over and that it had nothing to do with him. He would say "Mom, you must be anxious" and give me a hug.

Imagine if he kept those thoughts to himself! That's the sort of thing that can escalate over time. This is why it is vital to state what we think is obvious—that we love our kids and that we enjoy their company. Our facial expressions may not always convey what we think they do.

Communicating with our kids when we are overwhelmed is something that not only helps them understand they are free from trouble but also gives us an opportunity to show them how we deal with life's stressors. In the previous example, a simple hug cut my anxiety in half.

When we model being transparent about our emotional states, our teens will likely follow our lead. They will more likely voice when they are experiencing feelings of overwhelm and reach out to us. When they reach out to us, they're developing a coping skill that they will see has benefits over a lifetime.

Address and Acknowledge the Role of Mental Health

Historically, societies have neglected mental health treatment. Mental health has often been misunderstood or gone unacknowledged and undiscussed due to stigma. One silver lining of the COVID-19 pandemic was how it clarified that anyone can struggle with mental health issues and that it is vital to take care of one's mental health.

It is important to have awareness about your own mental health. Your well-being impacts everyone at home—including your teens. Your mental health may affect how you connect with your teen, so being forthright about it can help clear up assumptions your teen may be making (such as believing they are the cause of your issues). Share your situation in a way that lets them know what's going on but doesn't put the onus on your teen to be responsible for how you are doing. Getting help sets a good example. It shows your teen you are willing to seek help and reassures them you are handling what's going on. They see it is okay to ask for help.

Parents' use of substances (weed, alcohol, illicit or prescription drugs) can make children and teens feel unsafe and uncomfortable. The use of substances creates a barrier to connecting with your teen. You aren't truly present when you are on something. Whatever you do to cope with your mental health and stress, teens know. You may think you are hiding it from them, but you aren't. It is imperative to seek help if you are struggling with substance use.

Learn about Family Genetic History and Let Teens Know

Genetic history is important for you to know and for your teen as well. You or they might realize, "I didn't know that depression ran in our family. I feel better knowing that it just isn't me!"

Some parts of mental well-being are out of your control. So please release any shame that surfaces. Just as genetics can cause physical issues for you, genetics can cause mental health struggles. Regardless of the cause, parents still need to take steps to address issues that surface. Much can be managed through exercise, nutrition, psychotherapy, medicines, and other protocols and regimes. You can be the one to help break the negative cycle of not seeking help, whether mental health issues in your family history surfaced as nurture or nature.

Takeaway: Emotional Awareness Adds Vocabulary to the Language of Connectedness

The next time you notice something like "My chest is tight. I am thinking I can't get this all done right now. I am feeling overwhelmed. I am stressed. I want to shut down, check out, and move away," see those thoughts and feelings as an opportunity to pause and self-reflect. If you look at bodily sensations, action tendencies, thoughts, and feelings as a feedback loop system, they can serve as guiding principles in the ability to communicate.

The best way to stay connected to your teen is to stay emotionally regulated and present to your own experience. Looking within and noticing your physical sensations, emotions, thoughts, and feelings can help you feel grounded in the moment. As a result, you'll gain more confidence that you can handle the situation.

The next chapter breaks down *what's really happening between you and your teen* when you communicate. This topic is what most likely brought you to this book! Having undergone the self-reflection process, you are now better equipped to see what's really happening by slowing down to analyze if you are volleying.

Chapter 5 Reflection: Introspection

- Am I aware of my body sensations when interacting with others?
- What are my action tendencies (do I tend to flee, fight, freeze, fawn)?
- What is my internal dialogue saying? Are my thoughts mostly positive or negative?
- How do my thoughts impact how I feel and my interactions?
- How do my action tendencies impact my interactions?
- How do my coping mechanisms affect my interactions with my teen?

Exercise: Tackling Negative Self-Talk

Jot down your self-talk over the next couple of days. After understanding what's going on in your head, try this process when you have a negative thought:

1. *Pause. Acknowledge the thought:* "Here are those unwanted thoughts" or "I am being unkind to myself again."

2. *Stand up for yourself:* "I am not going to beat myself up."

3. *Give yourself some compassion and reassurance:* "I deserve to be nice to myself," or "I am okay." Replace a negative thought with a positive, kind version: "I am not a total failure; I just messed up." Say something you like about yourself.

4. *Distract:* Switch things up to break the negative pattern and prevent spiraling. Turn on your favorite song, change the scenery by heading outside, pick up a book, call a friend.

Modify any statements above with those that fit better for you, keeping the process the same. Remember, just because a thought comes into your head doesn't mean it is valid. Your inner voice may reflect insecurities, past messages received from your family of origin, echoes of a past coach's voice, or even something dating back to a bad experience in seventh grade. This process can help create distance between you and your negative thoughts. You can teach your teen to do the same.

Exercise: Using Breath to Regulate Emotions

Instead of moving to control the situation, regulate and calm yourself (body and mind) by pausing. You can create space and reset your nervous system with breath. Try 5-2-8 breathing:

1. Focus your eyes on one spot or close them and close your mouth.

2. Feel your feet on the ground or back in a chair.

3. Now inhale through your nose for five counts.

4. Hold the inhale at the top for two counts.

5. Exhale through your nose for eight counts.

6. Slightly constrict the back of your throat, making a sound like the ocean.

7. Repeat for three minutes and feel the rhythm of your breath. You can visualize the waves in the ocean while breathing. The exhale is key in calming the body. Even taking in two rounds of deep breathing will help you in the moment. Thirty seconds can change how you feel and the course of interaction between you and your teen. Don't forget to count.

CHAPTER 6

Between

*What's Going on between You and Your Teen—
from Trigger to Volley*

Embracing the Shift from Dependence to Interdependence

Children start out in life 100 percent dependent on their parents. As they grow, young children seek to distinguish themselves from parents, developing their own identity while staying close and becoming less dependent over time. Their early bids for independence may include, for example, running to the playground and jumping into the sandbox with a friend while parents remain a hundred feet away. As years pass, kids seek to extend this invisible cord over and over.

Differentiation and individuation are simply a part of growing up. However, such healthy growth on a teen's part can bring chaos to home life if a parent doesn't see such changes as natural. Healthy development requires caregivers to change how they parent with developmental milestones in mind.

Adolescence Requires Developing a "Sense of Agency"

Everyone wants a sense of agency—the ability to act freely and govern their own lives. It makes perfect sense that teens want a say or power in directing their lives, just as all people do.

Think about a teen's typical day. Much is out of their control. An alarm tells them when to rise. Bells ring to usher them between classes. They are told when to eat. They often must ask permission to go to the bathroom. They are required to take classes, some of which they have no interest or natural ability to perform in. They have little to no say in much of their day.

With after-school activities, many students are putting in up to twelve-hour days. They rise around 6:30 a.m., go to school for seven hours, work or take extracurriculars for a couple of hours, and then do homework for approximately two hours per night, often isolated in their room. This leaves teens feeling not only exhausted but micromanaged.

It is easy to relate to that feeling. When wishes aren't acknowledged, people fight for control, seeking greater autonomy. This leads to behaviors that look like tantrums—making outbursts, pitching demands, staging protests. Rebellion.

Dropping an Outdated Concept: Strike the Word Rebellion from Your Vocabulary

When googling parenting advice on the internet, as some parents do, well-intentioned help may lead us in the wrong direction. Here's a common misperception with defining what's going on with teens: "Rebellion is a natural part of being a teenager and growing up. By rebelling against authority, teenagers are expressing their beliefs and preferences as a distinct person separate from their parents."[1]

Teenage *individuation* is a natural part of growing up. When teens voice opinions about how to live their lives, they are standing on the bridge to adulthood. If a teen's natural growth process is to differentiate and individuate, why call it rebellion? It does not serve parents or teens well to think of adolescence this way—using the terms *rebellion* and *rebellious*, which have such negative connotations.

Labeling a teen as rebellious leaves little room for parents' curiosity, acceptance, compassion, empathy, and understanding. It creates a faulty lens that surely won't allow parents to see their teen in a positive light. These labels cause disconnection when communicating with your teen. Tension is built. Trust is splintered. Teens may rise up and/or shut down in response.

It's true that if teens aren't receiving enough positive attention from their parents, they will find other ways to get attention—positive or negative. However, labeling all behaviors that aren't "happy" as "rebellion" causes parents to miss important signals. When acting unhappy, your teen may be hurting in some way. Teens who have been labeled rebellious say things like "I feel like my parents always assume the worst in me. I don't feel like I ever get the benefit of the doubt."

Young kids do not yet have the language ability to express uncomfortable feelings on the inside, so they may express feelings through their behaviors, externally. In preschool, kids act out by hitting and biting. In elementary school, a child might try to bully another classmate. Daycare providers and teachers see biting, hitting, and bullying not simply as kids "behaving badly" but as telling signs that something else may be going on for that child. Teens rising up or closing off tells us something may be going on for them.

Teens have the developmental capability to vocalize much more than a young child, but two conditions must exist for teens to express what's happening inside them. The first condition is an open environment. As discussed, parents themselves must model verbal expression of feelings and emotions. This normalizes the openness of feelings: "This is how we talk at home." It also serves as teachable moments of what's happening emotionally within all of us. Feelings can be confusing and complicated. Discussing them openly sends the message "It's okay to have all the feelings. We deal with them by talking to each other." The second condition is safety. Only when there is safety established in the parent-child relationship can a teen be transparent about what is happening on the inside. These go hand in hand.

Daily, teens face new experiences and challenges. New feelings go along with these new experiences. When the home environment is one that is open to sharing all feelings and talking about difficult topics, it will feel natural for teens to share.

Using the following analogy can be helpful: We're advised to let a faucet drip when it is freezing outside or when there is too much pressure or stress on the pipe. Letting a bit out at a time ensures that the pipe won't burst and flood the room. Similarly, when parents stay open with their teen to allow feelings to be shared regularly, it is a release that brings relief. The room won't get completely flooded.

If teens aren't able to discuss their feelings, they may be letting you know something is wrong in other ways. Your teen may be having trouble with a friend, having difficulty finding their group, feeling overwhelmed with school, or feeling upset with something at home. There could also be a real mental health issue or an undiagnosed learning disability that is causing stress.[2] If you have the impression your teen is just being rebellious in this case, you most likely will start the interaction off with faulty assumptions, resulting in your teen not feeling you understand or you care to understand them. They also won't feel respected, which is foundational in any relationship. The interaction will lead to more disconnection and conflict than healthy and helpful connection. This leaves a teen to deal with not only their issues by themselves but also the added heavy feelings of not being in a good place with their parents.

Parents should lean in, ask questions, be patient, and remain calm instead of assuming a teen is just rebelling. Teens may actually feel it is the end of the world when things go south with a friend, if they mess up, or as they experience disappointment. A parent being there to listen instead of discounting how upsetting it feels for them will decrease their out-of-control, world-is-ending feelings. Dismissiveness increases uncomfortable feelings and furthers the spiral they may be experiencing.

As discussed, you can co-regulate your teen through your own calming presence and by just listening, empathizing, validating, and responding empathetically both verbally and nonverbally. Parents modeling this behavior teach teens self-regulating skills. When parents use *rebellious* to describe a teen's behavior, they may feel their teen does things "to them" on purpose. This compounds a negative cycle of interaction.

Parents' sensitivity to teens' need for autonomy requires a commitment. While understanding their prefrontal cortex is still developing, parents balance requested bids for freedom while looking out for poor choices made impulsively. The maturation process is a learning curve for both teen and parent. Open conversations with give-and-take exchanges help teens see parents' efforts moving them toward greater freedom. Good relations between parents and adolescents lessen the likelihood that teens will exhibit problem behaviors.[3]

Eric: Coping with Stress at Home

When Eric was a fourteen-year-old high school freshman, his parents sent him in for counseling. During the intake process, his parents expressed concern that he was being defiant at home. He would erupt periodically during interactions with his parents. They didn't understand the reason for the eruptions and just assumed it was teenage angst and rebellion. I asked Eric's parents what the atmosphere was like at home. They described some marital conflict.

When Eric came in for his first session, he described a version of home life that was a little different. He talked about the daily conflict at home between his two parents—not just yelling but screaming. He said, "They just don't get along, and it's constant."

He also described his struggles in his social world. He was having a tough time finding his friend group. It seemed the transition from middle school to high was harder than he thought it would be. Some of his friends were venturing into risky behaviors, including shoplifting. He didn't want to partake but felt stuck. He didn't want to lose his friends. His school was large, and it was hard to meet people. If he didn't have his current friends, he worried he would have no friends. He also described being frustrated with his parents still granting him only the same privileges and freedoms he had when he was in sixth grade. This made it difficult in his social world.

I asked Eric what he did to cope with the stress of his parents arguing at home and the pressures of social life at school. He said, "I think back to when things were calmer at home. I think of when my mom used to take me to the ice cream shop."

Underneath Eric's anger (or, as his parents saw, rebellion) were multiple stressors. He was frustrated with his parents yelling and home life feeling chaotic. He was struggling with finding his people at school. He was embarrassed among his peers about his lack of freedom.

Eric would vacillate between isolating in his room and being angry and confrontational when interacting with his parents. His parents assumed he was just being defiant and an "out-of-control teen."

I had a few sessions with Eric's parents about the level of conflict at home. I suggested a couples counselor. They chose not to move forward with couples counseling and were unsuccessful in decreasing their marital conflict.

The stress at home continued for Eric. Connection with his parents was strained. During a session with Eric, he mentioned his parents put him on an antidepressant, which is usually something the therapist, parent, psychiatrist, and client discuss.

Eric was the identified patient, labeled as the "rebellious" teenager. Yet the story went deeper than that.

Understanding Dependence and Interdependence in Parenting

Teens want to shift from pure dependence on you (where you make all their decisions for them) to interdependence (where they have a voice and you work together). They begin to view decisions as personal choices. They want to make them on their own—or at least be included in making them.

The process of developing interdependence often feels like a push-and-pull effect. Teens push parents away by saying, "I don't need you; I got this." Then they pull back, saying, "I am scared; I don't know if I can do it" or "I messed up; I need you back." This is typical and a healthy phase of development.

You'll notice that definitions of rebellion commonly use the word *authority*—for example, "rebelling against authority." If your style of parenting is authoritarian, it entails high expectations, frequent punishments, and little nurturing. As discussed in chapter 4, this style of parenting, demanding adherence, will likely backfire during the teenage years.

An authoritarian parenting style invites misdiagnosed "rebellion." Teenagers need to express their feelings, opinions, and discomfort in the relationship. The result of teens sharing may cause conflict and disconnection. Parents must consider that teens are in a developmental stage of differentiating, individuating, and seeking autonomy. Teens continually need the security of a parent's acceptance, love, and support—even through differing opinions and amid their mistakes.

If you tend to be a helicopter, snowplow, or lawnmower parent, your overinvolvement leaves little room for a teen's much-needed personal space. When a parent isn't respectful of a teen's privacy, it can upset the teen. Teens who need space say things like "She keeps just walking in on me and doesn't even knock!"

Overinvolvement can send the message that you don't think your teen is capable. A teen may say of his dad, "He checks in with me four times a night, asking if I am studying. It ends up in a blowup. I just feel he is constantly on me, and I do have straight As."

Both scenarios invite pushback, conflict, and what has been historically termed rebellion on a teen's part.

Interdependence requires mutual reliance. Teens rely on their parents more; they need financial support, food, and shelter. Parents ideally rely on teens to share feelings, thoughts, and opinions. Shared knowledge happens through open communication and collaboration.

Think of getting a promotion. You may not be given full access or the full scope of your responsibilities right away. You still rely on those with more expertise and experience than you. As you slowly venture into this new realm, you seek information and insights. You expect colleagues to welcome your questions—to hear and answer you. Long-term, interdependent relationships must be managed. Even once you become proficient in your new role, you still need the full support of your team. Teens rely on their parents to help them gain proficiency as they learn to hold the reins of their own life. If you let them lead during the adolescent years and you follow close behind, when you have to take the reins for a bit, they will value and trust your opinion.

Potential Patterns between You and Your Teen

Throughout this book, you have explored communication techniques, parenting approaches, and attachment styles with an eye toward finding potential solutions and overcoming potential barriers to each. You have investigated your family of origin, bearing in mind your tendencies. All these factors impact the cycle of interaction—the patterns—between you and your teen. In fact, the influence of your family of origin and the pattern of interaction that existed between you and your primary caregivers may mirror what's happening between you and your teen now. At least, such reflections provide clues to what's going on.

In any relationship, patterns appear when the environment feels tense, when disagreements arise, or during times of stress. Unhealthy communication and reactiveness cause distress, bringing the relationship to a place of disconnection and repeated negative interactions. These cycles will likely repeat until addressed.

Each person in a relational dyad (including parents and teens) reacts to insecurity in the relationship differently. Each person creates defenses to protect themselves. Such reactions are each person's attempt to figure out how to navigate the interaction.

Each person involved must shoulder responsibility to create a healthier dynamic. The following is a process to help break down the interaction. This can help you further understand what might be happening between you and your teen.

Breaking Down Your Repeated Pattern of Interaction

Have you ever noticed that sometimes the cycle of interaction is the same in every conversation with your teen, only the content has changed? The cycle runs through triggers, physiological reactions/emotions, action tendencies, thoughts, feelings, and defenses. There is some debate about the order these take place. Nonetheless, these patterns exist. Breaking down the pattern will lead you to better "volley" with your teen—to find a rhythm that works for both of you.

Cycle of Response

Once a trigger ignites a physiological response, the following patterned thoughts, feelings, and behaviors play out in a cycle (for each of you!).

Unfortunately, with those closest to us, defenses used can set off additional triggers. Patterns of interaction can be summarized as "You do this, and I think and feel this way, so then I do that, and you react." Round and round it goes.

Let's go back to the story of Bobby and his mother from chapter 3. What wasn't shared previously is that their pattern of interaction resurfaces over and over in their relationship.

Stepping away from the content and processing each person's internal experience—and what's happening between each other—helps distill the ongoing pattern of interaction. Once sorted out, it is easier to identify and address what's really going on and ultimately break the cycle.

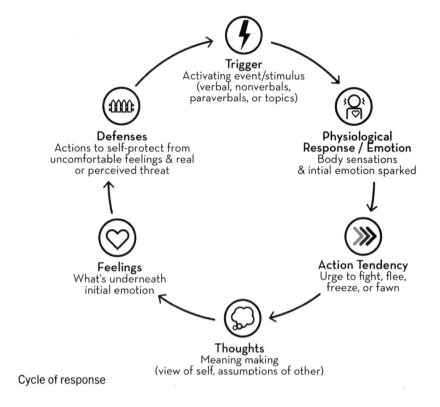

Cycle of response

Triggers and Reactions between Bobby and His Mom

When Bobby's mother (Jen) is faced with something she can't give him, whether it's a need or a want, her head gets hot, and she gets angry. Her urge is to fight. Her thoughts tend to go to a negative place, telling herself that she is disappointing her son and that he thinks she is a bad mom for not providing for him. She is showing that she is angry at her son, but underneath her anger, she is embarrassed and sad. These feelings are uncomfortable for her. In her family of origin, these more vulnerable feelings were not expressed by her parents, and she was not invited to express them.

Her son never sees this part of her. In dealing with her uncomfortable feelings, she pushes her son away by criticizing him. She wants to end the interaction, so she shuts down his request with a no. Bobby's mother goes through the same process anytime she is met with not being able to give Bobby something he needs or wants.

When Bobby senses his mother isn't happy (through her verbal, nonverbal, or paraverbal communication), he gets frustrated. He may or may not know if he is the cause of her annoyance, but he grows uncomfortable and anxious. His stomach knots, and he feels the urge to flee.

His thoughts go to a dark place as he tells himself he is "a bother" to his mother—that he isn't good enough in some way. Sad and disappointed, he knows he is doing something that is upsetting his mother. He hides these feelings from her because they don't share how they really feel with each other. He feels anxious and shuts down. He then shuts his mother out. Bobby goes through the same process anytime he senses his mother is annoyed or unhappy. He assumes fault for his mother's state of mind.

The content of their patterned arguments may change, but the cycle is the same for Bobby and his mother. The trigger is activated when his mother senses she can't meet Bobby's needs or wants and when Bobby senses his mother's unhappiness.

Focus on the Volley with Your Teen to Avoid Negative Patterns

Remembering that the parent-child volley starts at infancy, you can see how you met their security-seeking overtures over and over again. Your responses satisfied their needs and calmed their distress, creating security. The infant instinctively feels "My parents are right here with me."

This volley built trust and a secure bond. In a sense, your infant felt seen, heard, understood, comforted, and reassured by you. Now the volley with your teen consists of different tasks to provide them with those same feelings. This kind of connection feels good for both parents and children.

As your child becomes a teen, the volley becomes less labor intensive and more emotionally intensive. With secure attachment during adolescence, the "serve-return" consistency is achieved through parents' attunement, sensitivity, and emotional

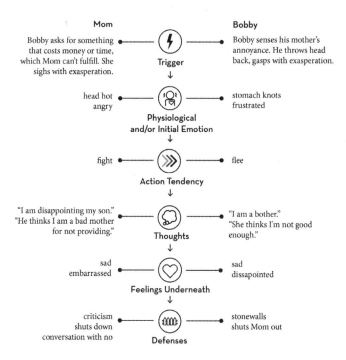

Mom   Bobby

Bobby asks for something   ⚡   Bobby senses his mother's
that costs money or time,   annoyance. He throws head
which Mom can't fulfill. She   Trigger   back, gasps with exasperation.
sighs with exasperation.   ↓

head hot   😠   stomach knots
angry   frustrated
                            Physiological
                          and/or Initial Emotion
                                     ↓

fight   »»   flee

                            Action Tendency
                                     ↓

"I am disappointing my son."   💭   "I am a bother."
"He thinks I am a bad mother   "She thinks I'm not good
for not providing."   Thoughts   enough."
                                     ↓

sad   ♡   sad
embarrassed   dissapointed
                          Feelings Underneath
                                     ↓

criticism   🪗   stonewalls
shuts down   shuts Mom out
conversation with no   Defenses

Patterned responses in action

closeness. The volley now features verbal and nonverbal exchanges—back and forth—with feelings attached.

The volley takes much more thought and intention, noticing your internal experience while staying connected to your teen. You must be curious and listen to gain understanding. Even when you may not agree, show empathy and validate their feelings. This back-and-forth volley brings comfort, reassurance, and closeness to the relationship—creating trust and safety. Ultimately, a secure bond allows for more transparency and an ongoing feeling of connectedness. The teen once again feels, as they did in infancy, "I am not alone; my parents are right here with me."

When you imagine volleying in any sport (tennis, ping-pong, volleyball, pickleball), you envision a slow and rhythmic pace. You are serving at a certain arch so that the other can easily return the ball. There is a cadence, a cooperative back and forth, in taking turns returning the ball to the other. As you learn to volley, you and your teen can more easily express your emotions and share your thoughts and feelings with reciprocity.

The ball is the message you are sending over the net to reach the other person. The ball is your current experience. It is filled with your thoughts and feelings that are served up and volleyed to each other. The goal is to keep the ball in play and continue the volley. You aren't keeping score. No one is out to win because you are on the same team. If you drop the ball or hit it out of bounds, you self-correct by acknowledging and apologizing so you can easily restart the rhythm of the volley. There is an ease of play and trust that the other is there to learn how to volley with you.

Sometimes the volley gets interrupted by misunderstandings, defensiveness, lack of attunement, and absence of empathy. These can feel like a charging of the net, sudden aggressive line drives, deceptive drop shots, or someone dropping the ball and walking off the court. The other player may think, "I thought we were on the same team." "I didn't think we were keeping score." "I guess I need to have better defense." "I need to start serving aces across the net." Anything that departs from simply volleying back and forth causes disconnection, and the volley comes to a halt.

You Have the Power to Change the Course of the Volley

What moment do you as a parent know you can change the course of interaction—the moment they toss something over that challenges you, triggers you, or causes you discomfort?

You can direct the ball in play. This is best done by *slowing down*. Pause, take a few breaths, use your curiosity to understand what is happening for your teen, and empathize. If you are less reactionary, there is less tendency to jump into a negative cycle. This absolutely can change the course of interaction. It also will create safety and facilitate understanding for both parent and teen. Please keep in mind you are the teacher in the skills of volleying.

Let's take one more look at Bobby and his mom. This time, see how a volley can change habitual responses.

Interactional Model

Changing Patterned Responses

Step 1. Notice by slowing down and sensing what is going on within yourself and between you and your teen. See the pattern and adjust instinctive responses.

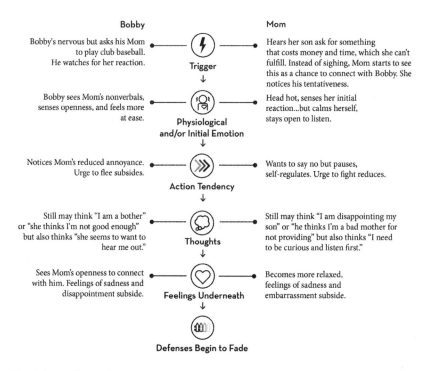

Bobby

Bobby's nervous but asks his Mom to play club baseball. He watches for her reaction.

Bobby sees Mom's nonverbals, senses openness, and feels more at ease.

Notices Mom's reduced annoyance. Urge to flee subsides.

Still may think "I am a bother" or "she thinks I'm not good enough" but also thinks "she seems to want to hear me out."

Sees Mom's openness to connect with him. Feelings of sadness and disappointment subside.

Mom

Hears her son ask for something that costs money and time, which she can't fulfill. Instead of sighing, Mom starts to see this as a chance to connect with Bobby. She notices his tentativeness.

Head hot, senses her initial reaction...but calms herself, stays open to listen.

Wants to say no but pauses, self-regulates. Urge to fight reduces.

Still may think "I am disappointing my son" or "he thinks I'm a bad mother for not providing" but also thinks "I need to be curious and listen first."

Becomes more relaxed, feelings of sadness and embarrassment subside.

Trigger

Physiological and/or Initial Emotion

Action Tendency

Thoughts

Feelings Underneath

Defenses Begin to Fade

Changing patterned responses

With sensitivity to what's happening internally, you can better approach the volley with a calm and open presence.

Step 2. Listen to understand. *Step 3. Respond* by confirming, empathizing, validating, and own and repair with sincerity.

In using the interactional model, your teen will be watching your changed reactions. Teens learn from you and will learn from you to change their reactions as well. Open and transparent dialogues about thoughts and feelings help clear up assumptions that cause conversations to get off track and create disconnection. Action tendencies and defenses—will fade over time as you and your teen feel greater trust and security that your volleys will be returned in good faith.

You can see the outcome of your repeated patterns can be totally different with even a small shift. Notice how Mom feels the same on the inside and retains her parenting decision while changing her external reaction to be more empathetic. Rather than a harsh "No!" she allows Bobby to share how he is thinking and feeling. She empathizes

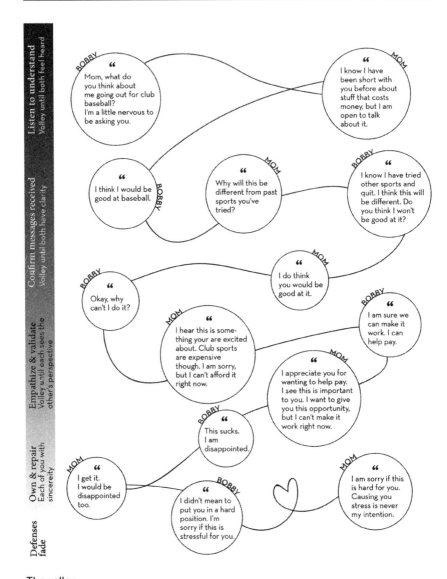

The volley

and validates; Bobby then feels heard and understood by his mother. She also feels heard and understood by Bobby.

To keep the volley going, see additional phrases on "Ideas to Keep the Volley Going" chart. These can help you each gather a better understanding of the other's thoughts, feelings, and position. These are broken down by each step in the instinctive response pattern.

Ideas to keep the volley going

Trigger

Questions	"I noticed you sighed. Can you tell me what is happening?" "I noticed a look on your face. Is everything okay?"
Responses	"I get upset when we _____." "I have a hard time when we _____."

Physiological response / initial emotion

Questions	"I sense something is wrong. Can you tell me what's up?" "I notice you seem _____. Is that right?"
Responses	"I feel tense/uncomfortable in my _____." "My body feels _____." "My initial feeling is _____."

Action tendency

Questions	"I notice you seem distant/angry/sad. Can you tell me what's going on?" "I sense we might be headed to an argument. Can we slow things down?" "Can we slow things down? I don't want to get sideways with you."
Responses	"My initial reaction is to _____ right now." "I want to _____, but I am going to calm myself and try to stay here and talk through this with you."

Thinking

Questions	"Can you tell me what you're thinking?" "What are you saying to yourself about what's happening between us right now?" "I am open to hearing what you're thinking. Can you tell me what's up?"
Responses	"I tell myself you're thinking _____ about me." "I tell myself I am _____."

Feeling

Questions	"How are you feeling? I promise I am open to listening." "I want to know how you are feeling. Can you tell me more about what's going on?"
Responses	"I show that I am _____, but underneath, I am really feeling _____." "I am feeling _____ because I/we _____."

Confirming, empathizing, and validating

Responses	"My understanding is that you're saying/needing/wanting _____. Is that right?" "I hear you are feeling _____. Am I getting that right?" "I understand you are feeling _____. That sounds painful." "That sounds hard. How can I help?" "I think I understand how you're feeling. That must be tough." "I am sorry you are feeling _____. I am always here to listen." "I know it is hard when _____. I get it."

If there is conflict

Responses	"I am sorry for _____ [my part in the conflict]." "I see I hurt your feelings, and I feel bad about that." "I understand I hurt your feelings. That is never my intention. I am truly sorry."

Basically, any time you have the impulse to share an old-school parenting line like "No, end of discussion" or "Go to your room," you can instead draw on empathy and phrases like those above to change the outcome.

Parents can't give teens everything they want; that's not helpful either. The answer no will still be the answer to their requests sometimes. However, when you recognize the situation (and your no) is tough for them, they gain respect for you and learn how to hear and accept that answer. Rather than fighting you, they can let down their guard and learn from you. They'll find out not just how to deal with not getting what they want but—more importantly—how to have healthy interactions when things don't go their way.

Story: Dropping My Son Off at College

When I was dropping my son off for college, it stirred many emotions for both of us. For him, it was a mixture of sadness, worry, and much excitement. For me, it was mainly sadness and anxiety about leaving him. I wondered if he was ready, if I had taught him everything I wanted to, and whether he was going to be able to live on his own. Could I be okay without seeing him every day? Should I cry in front of him? If he cried, should I tell him he didn't have to stay?

My anxiety got the best of me as we rushed from store to store, gathering items he needed for his dorm room. I was quite uncomfortable internally and most likely looked panicked and/or angry. I was short in my responses, and I grew exasperated. This got us entangled.

He sensed something was wrong with me. He got uncomfortable and frustrated and didn't know what to do. Perhaps inevitably, we got into an argument. It lasted about one minute. Then we both stopped and said, "This is hard, leaving each other." Being able to witness the difficulty of the moment calmed us both.

Takeaway: Slow Down, Analyze the Volley

Parents model lessons on how to express and share emotions. You teach your teen self-regulation, healthy conflict, and how to do the relationship thing. It takes intention and effort to look at the cycle of interaction. Understand the patterns that exist and what is happening both within yourself and between you and your teen. When trust is built, there is safety in being transparent with each other. Feelings can be expressed, understanding can unfold, and empathy can be delivered back to the other person. It's a volley.

The next chapter looks at external influences—the "static" or noise from outside forces that may be creating disconnection and stress for you and your teen. You can build strategies to shore up your family bonds despite the 24/7 news cycle, social media, smartphones, and more.

Chapter 6 Reflection: Looking Between

- What are the patterns between you and your teen?
- Recall a recent negative interaction with your teen.
- Consider your patterns of interaction—trigger, physiological response, action tendency, thoughts, feelings, defenses.
- Imagine your teen's answers as well.
- Once you've done this exercise for one interaction, you'll be better able to spot where you both may be "serving aces," "charging the net," or "dropping the ball" during the parent-teen volley going forward.
- Explore the "Ideas to Keep the Volley Going" table.
- Consider if you are filtering interactions through a "rebellious teen" lens. Ask, Is my teen really "rebelling" or simply signaling to me that something is wrong?

CHAPTER 7

External Influences That Cause Stress and Disconnection

Today many external influences and numerous addictive distractions cause disconnection in the parent-teen relationship. Life stress seems to be increasing daily for both parents and teens.

Society's embedded use of technology accelerates the already fast pace of life. The avenues to mentally "check out" have increased, interrupting much-needed face-to-face interaction between parent and teen and among the whole family unit. Teens face new pressures by simply being a teen in the present day. These factors create exhaustion in all of us.

It seems everyone lives under the mantra of "Do more and do it faster." Little time is left to promote in-person togetherness and human connection. A sense of belonging has almost been lost to smartphones rather than to those closest to us—in person. While it seems like we're hyperconnected, technology actually promotes isolation in our own homes. It is an intrusion, taking away the time and contact needed to build trust with one another in our relationships.

Families no longer seem to make one another a priority. Everyone becomes distracted by whatever may be waiting online for us—something or someone better, we think. This gives limited time to connect with one another face-to-face. If someone were continually ringing the doorbell at home, would family members welcome everyone in, including strangers?

People get a momentary "high" (a dopamine hit) from likes, comments, and messages. The feeling is short lived, though, as each person anticipates even more likes from the next post, story, reel, tweet, or thread. The time spent swept away online takes individuals away from cultivating relationships at home. Working on family relationships and liking each other takes a back seat to getting online likes.

According to Johann Hari, author of *Stolen Focus*, human attention spans have shortened.[1] When listening to another person talk, even in person, people tend to want the abbreviated version. How can families attend to one another's emotional well-being when wishing for an abbreviated "sound bite" of the issue?

Everyone knows when someone isn't paying attention and is on their phone and simply not present. Trying to talk to someone who is looking down, tapping a screen, and not making eye contact evokes a certain feeling. You may think, "I am ready to talk to you; why aren't you ready to talk to me?" You can become infuriated, thinking, "Please give me some attention!" Yet everyone takes turns doing this to the other. Each feels justified in the moment.

Parents' Work Lives Now

The lines between work and home life have become blurred. Working remotely and working from home have been rising trends for decades, accelerated by a global pandemic and technological trends.

Employers expect employees to be available wherever they are, at all hours of the day. In a sense, everyone is carrying their office around with them. Everyone feels behind, even after a twelve-hour workday. It seems there is always one more thing that could be done to catch up or to try to get ahead. Just one more email or call to make. If you have two minutes, you feel you can fit it in.

Technology was supposed to make lives easier, streamline processes, and create more efficiency. Yet it seems like technology is making individuals work more.

People are constantly multitasking to get more and more done despite evidence that multitasking isn't actually all that effective. Earl Miller, a neuroscientist at MIT and one of the world's experts on divided attention, says that human brains are "not wired to multitask well. . . . When people think they're multitasking, they're actually just switching from one task to another very rapidly. And every time they do, there's a cognitive cost in doing so."[2]

Beyond the cognitive costs, multitasking today carries the emotional costs of losing face-to-face connection with others as attention gets divided among screens.

Working from home "after hours" often interrupts or prevents family time. This costs mom and dad time they could have spent growing their relationship. It costs parents time spent bonding with kids. Negotiating time spent online causes conflict. Countless times a day, conversations with spouses and teens begin with "Could you get off the phone/screen/game?"

Estimates say people touch their phones over two thousand times a day. "Roughly six-in-ten parents say they spend too much time on their smartphone," and at least "68% of parents say they at least sometimes feel distracted by their phone when spending time with their kids."[3]

One result of increased screen use is a lack of parent-teen face-to-face interaction. Teens in therapy have said things like "I ask my mom for time, but she is always busy. I don't want to burden her with scheduling time with me to hang out" or "I watch my parents at night sit at opposite ends of the couch on their phones. No one is talking to each other."

Less time spent with parents and more time with others (including those we don't know) means external influences add more stress to family members' lives. External factors can make parenting more difficult. The tendency is for less mom/dad time than parenting time. However, in light of teens' typical life pressures, more than ever, they need their parents to be a grounding force in their lives. Parents can help teens cope, bringing calm and comfort.

Modern Pressures: Screens Add Stress for Teens

Teens today are exposed to more external influences (outside of the home) than in past generations. With busy lives and demanding school and extracurricular schedules, teens spend ample time away from their parents both online and offline. Teens often spend more time with coaches and teachers than parents each week. Online they are highly visible and can watch and communicate with . . . *anyone*.

It can feel a bit unnerving. Parents constantly wonder, "Who and what is influencing my teen?" and "Do I have a handle on who and what they are exposed to?" We may feel we are walking on a tightrope again, questioning how much we should try to control what they are doing and seeing. If we get involved, are we being nosey? Or just being a good parent? It is hard to wrap your arms around it all.

Teen life today includes many of the same challenges as we had growing up; they navigate peer pressure, social hierarchy, physical transitions, mass confusion, and impulsivity. Yet there are even more challenges now. High-level pressure stems from numerous sources: peers, parents (real or perceived), teachers, coaches, and social media. Modern expectations for teenagers' lives are generally out of sync for someone at their age and developmental state. The current status quo can feel overwhelming to teens.

How Life Has Changed in Just Two Decades

Sometime over the last ten to twenty years, the idea that people should "produce more, achieve more, and *be more*, right now" has yielded a level of pressure for teens that I have never seen before.

I have a clear vantage point, being a therapist working with teens for two decades and a parent of children ranging in age from twenty-five years to ten years old. I sit with teens every day and hear the word *pressure* a lot. I also hear "It's too late for me. I can't go out for soccer because I will embarrass myself. Why didn't my parents sign me up when I was five?" That was from a thirteen-year-old eighth grader.

In looking back at what my twenty-five-year-old was doing in both academics and extracurriculars a decade ago, the expectations differ vastly now. For parents with kids entering middle school and high school, I am sure it seems as though this is simply how it has always been. However, this high level of pressure and stress has been gradually escalating with each passing year.

Recognizing the New Academic and Extracurricular Pressures

Right now, it feels like teens entering high school (freshman year) are being asked to perform at the level of a college student, both academically and with extracurricular activities. Teens express they don't even know where the bar is set.

What is "enough"? The bar for accomplishment seems set in the clouds to begin with. Once they feel they have a finger on it, it's just thrown up higher. They feel they can never reach the standard. The "moving bar" makes it difficult for teens to take in their own accomplishments and feel good about themselves. This is during a time of development when a sense of accomplishment plays an integral role in building their self-esteem and self-worth.

The current environment leaves little room for trial and error, which is how teens (and all of us) learn. Teens worry that one bad grade will ruin their future. When it comes to academics, the early focus is on getting into a good college. They must get "good grades," but what constitutes a good grade has changed recently. When just comparing what was considered a good GPA in the past, a 4.0, to now, a 4.5, it's a big difference. Some say a 4.0 will close the door to some opportunities.[4] The pressure to perform at such a high level all the time doesn't allow for experimentation and growth. Instead, we're creating an unrealistic need for perfection.

Of course, some pressure and stress can be a beneficial force for growth. However, too much stress causes psychological distress, impacting mental health. The load each individual teen carries can vary, but it is important to know that stress feels different to teens than adults.

Teens have more impulsive behaviors and greater susceptibility to stress than adults. The brain region for reasoning matures later than the part that processes fear and anxiety. In the teenage years, the amygdala operates in overdrive, with less input from the rational, problem-solving frontal lobe. That makes stress seem much bigger and overwhelming.

The teenage brain's frontal lobes, which house executive functioning, are still developing. Teens are being asked to organize, stay on task, plan, juggle multiple tasks, problem-solve, and tolerate stress. Yet executive functioning of the brain isn't completely developed until the mid- to late twenties. Managing daily tasks may create more stress for adolescents than adults.[5]

Prioritizing Intrinsic Benefits of Sports

Playing sports during the adolescent years can pack in many intrinsic benefits. Playing sports can help individuals learn to work with others as a team. Sports can build self-esteem and teach kids how to set and work toward a goal. The benefits of playing sports also include strengthening physical and mental health, gaining a sense of belonging in a social group, and learning dedication, responsibility, how to deal with defeat, how to win graciously, and ideally how to feel a sense of achievement regardless of the score—to name a few positive aspects. Yet parents, coaches, and teens today often set their sights on a teen's college athletic scholarships or playing at a professional level.

The rate of high school athletes earning scholarships or "going pro" is low. According to the National Collegiate Athletics Association (NCAA), "Nearly eight million students currently participate in high school athletics in the United States. More than 480,000 compete as NCAA athletes, and just a select few within each sport move on to compete at the professional or Olympic level."[6] That means very few students go on to play at the college level. From a mental health perspective, it's important to balance the reality of advancement in sports with the level of pressure and performance we are asking of youth.

Considering the "Baseline Stress" for Each Teen

We all experience a baseline of stress from daily functioning. Yet for teens, the baseline also includes teenage social and emotional challenges. Teens today manage more media input than any teenage group in history. One teenage client said stress felt like hefty sandbags placed upon him. If a teen's home life fills with stress too, be it parental conflict (whether parents are together or divorced) or teen-parent relationship strife, the routine teenage stress can become unmanageable.

It is imperative that parents consider the meter of stress of their teen and not in comparison to other teens or siblings. Determine if current stress levels are promoting growth or potentially compromising a teen's mental health. Seek ways to alleviate stress rather than add pressure, and get professional help to sort out the stress as necessary.

Internet-Connected Activities: Phones, Screens, and Social Media

Time spent online provides a window into other worlds. The rise of portable screens (phones, iPads, game consoles) and associated social media apps and online interactions has created an entirely new context for parenting.

Teens already under stress feel the pressure magnified online. The level of pressure depends on what your teen is doing online and how they process what they see.

There is no need to unduly vilify social media, smartphones, or screens— because they have the capability to bring good things if we monitor their use. Teens can connect with their friends and family, finding a sense of community. They can provide ease in making plans and building relationships. Teens can find support and gain inspiration from what others post.

However, some very real downsides to social media have emerged, backed up by research findings about teens' mental health states.[7] Look out for signs of being overwhelmed and a heightened level of stress, and talk about managing stress with your teens even before you see a problem.

My Youngest Daughter's Story: Computers and "Influencers"

One year I had gotten a new laptop for work and decided to give my old one to my youngest. She was ten at the time. Day two after giving her my laptop, I noticed she was sitting at the kitchen table with her headphones plugged into the computer. Her previous screen time had usually been spent in the living room–kitchen area, where I could see and hear what she was viewing.

I asked her what she was watching. She replied, "Why do you need to know? It's not like it's an 'influencer' or anything."

My husband and I looked at each other in a bit of shock. I was taken aback that she had even heard the term *influencer*, let alone that she would use it as a point of debate.

I said to her, "We always want to know what you are watching. We want to make sure it's age appropriate. Anything and everything you are taking in actually influences you in some way."

It's true for all of us. Anything we look at is an influence.

She went back to watching her shows in the living room, where we could see, hear, and have dialogue around her choices.

Of course, once you hand your teen a phone with internet access, it becomes increasingly difficult to monitor their screen choices. We can't always know where they are scrolling.

Many apps exist to block teens' access to certain content and websites, which can help establish healthy boundaries. Equally important, teach your teens how to use their best instincts around phone use by setting expectations (ideally well before they have a phone and throughout their teen years).

Belonging Online: Overcoming Bullying, Harassment, Exclusion

As mentioned in chapter 2, belonging is a need all humans possess, and developmentally for teens, it is crucial to feel they belong in their social world. The adolescent years are largely about moving toward peers and finding their people. Not belonging in their social world is painful.

Social media is a constant discovery of belonging or not. What seems as simply sending a message to connect with someone can be met with heartache and confusion in how to navigate. Sending a message and seeing three little dots moving with no reply, sending a message and noticing it being unread, or being taken off someone's story leaves teens in a state of anxiousness and insecurity, questioning what action they should take next. The spiral can happen quickly: "No one responded to my text; it's been ten minutes." Or "No one read my story." Or "He/she read my story but didn't comment. No one wants to do anything with me. I have no friends."

When we weren't invited to a party before social media, we may have not even known. Maybe we'd hear about the event the next day. Now with social media, teens know with immediacy that they aren't included. They can also witness the event live or through photos. It is also obvious to others when they aren't included, causing embarrassment and sometimes shame. It feels like "I see I don't belong, and now everyone else sees it too."

Teens' desire to stay in nearly constant contact with their friends can become a stressful, time-consuming task. In a teen's mind, letting the Snapchat string go feels like they are jeopardizing their friendships and belonging to the group. (This may be their perception or a true concern.)

Social media makes it easy to harass and throw insecurities and cruelty at others. (And they surely don't see adults setting good examples of being kind to one another online.) A 2022 Pew Research Center survey found that "nearly half of U.S. teens ages 13 to 17 (46%) report ever experiencing at least one of six cyberbullying behaviors."[8]

The most common bullying behavior is name-calling, with spreading false rumors coming in second. With social media a 24/7 constant in their lives, there is no break from this treatment, and with the public nature of social media, humiliation can accompany it. Everyone can see the ill-treatment, causing overwhelming feelings of "No one likes me; I am out." Or even more painful, "No one cares to stick up for me."

Our survival stress response system activates in times of real or perceived danger. It can be hard for teens to feel settled while in a constant state of monitoring, mitigating, and avoiding rejection.

Avoid the Comparison Trap

Many of us who are now parents had negative experiences growing up when someone compared us to a neighbor's kid, a relative in the family, or a sibling. It never felt good.

Now this experience of comparison and falling short happens daily online. It affects some more than others, but the effects can become devastating for teens.

I often hear in my sessions with teens common themes. When they're describing what they've seen online, they say things like "I don't look like that," "I'm not doing that," or "I don't have anything figured out like they do."

Often this isn't even a true peer-to-peer comparison. They may be looking at someone decades older, with a staff. Social shares never show a true representation of someone's life, merely a snapshot, a highlight reel. It breeds an illusion of perfection. As you can imagine, constant comparison with other people's highlights can leave anyone feeling negative about themselves. This daily comparison trap can explode a teen's existing insecurities and create new ones.

Magnifying Insecurities: A Hyperfocus on Physical Appearance

What actually happens when teens scroll through images and videos? They are comparing physical appearances. This is during a time of rapid body changes and uncertainty about their place in the world.

- *Appearances online.* Teens tend to hyperfocus on their own insecurities while scrolling. For example, if you have an insecurity about the appearance of your nose, when you scroll on the internet, you will focus on the images of other people's noses. This intensifies your insecurities. Your nose will of course seem worse compared to someone who has taken a photo fifty times to get the right angle or who has used Photoshop, filters, and retouching apps.
- *Face-altering apps.* During a time when teens are already insecure about their appearance, these apps can now alter their appearance, showing them how they can "look better." This automatically plants a seed in an adolescent's mind such as "I don't look good the way I am," "I have more flaws than I realized," or "Beauty is unattainable."

Online scrolling can create unhealthy behaviors in a need for perfection in what they look like. They are evaluating their appearance countless times a day. One teen commented, "Even if I am not scrolling online, I still end up critiquing how I look. It's Snapchat; I take about forty pictures of myself every day and pick myself apart."

Teens are in the process of individuating and developing a sense of self, as discussed in chapters 2 and 6. Individuating provides teens an opportunity to build self-esteem and confidence in who they are uniquely. Endless exposure to others on social media makes them susceptible to interruptions of this process, which is vital to their development. Being bombarded with images of celebrities and influencers, interpreted by a teen as "who and how I should be," creates confusion and even distress. Instead of exploring and getting comfortable with themselves, teens constantly revisit their identities depending on what they view. The identity debate may even become a moment-to-moment internal discussion. They may not be able to truly discover who they are unless they can make the space to do so offline.

Talk with your teens about the thoughts and feelings that come up with the use of various media and devices. Ensure they ask themselves questions about how their use affects their mood and "view of self." With these things in mind, they can change who they follow depending on how they feel. This is learning for all of us!

Dating, Hookup Culture, and Media

Pop culture broadcasts hypersexualization and hookups to teens (and all of us) through music, TV, movies, and social media. Movies depict themes of no-strings-attached encounters and friends with benefits, glorifying the idea of sex without commitment. A "casual hookup" can mean anything from kissing to groping to oral or penetrative sex. Teens often follow this world of casual sex, whether they really want to or not.

While teenage sexual exploration is developmentally normative, the natural progression of sexual events changes when it comes to the pressures of hookups. For adolescents, sexual contact typically begins with holding hands, kissing, and touching over the clothes and then moves to oral and penetrative sex.[9] Hookups could be just kissing or full-on intercourse.

Research points to the influence of sexual content online: "Sexually explicit media exposure in early adolescence was strongly related to three risky sexual behaviors—early sexual debut, unsafe sex, and sexual partners—in late adolescence, and this relationship was very close to causal."[10]

Additionally, hookups come before the date now. Sexually active teens say things like "Dating is so hard to navigate; no one wants to put a label on anything" and "I can't ask if someone likes me, but we can get naked together. It seems so weird."

Teens (including middle schoolers) are graphic in nature, calling sex *f***ing*. It seems they are talking about something so normal, like heading to class or watching a movie, as they speak about the act of sex. Teens' access to social media and dating apps at such a young age has a tremendous impact and normalizes uncommitted sexual encounters. Yet teens don't really understand the emotional ramifications of engaging in such an intimate physical act.

There can be psychological consequences of being physically intimate with someone with no opportunity for emotional closeness. When one person ends up having feelings and the other one doesn't, it's felt as rejection (specifically emotional connection rejection).

Some know it's a hookup but hope for more: "I know it was a hookup, but I thought after sex, they would want to continue seeing me or at least hook up again. She never responded to my texts again. I feel so dismissed. Maybe I am just too much for anyone."

For others, feelings of shame and guilt can accompany hookups. Experiencing physical intimacy with someone but then getting ghosted after can impact your self-esteem. I hear things like "I felt good in the moment, but I felt worse afterward. I am embarrassed and have regrets. I hope no one finds out." Or "I wanted to feel close to someone, but I ended up in such distress afterward."

For those looking for a relationship, it can be confusing: "Am I only supposed to hook up? Do I tell the other person I am looking for a relationship, or will that seem pathetic?" Boys share they aren't sure if they should approach a girl, take them on a real date, open the door, or pay for a meal. Some want a committed relationship but avoid commitment because they say it's messy: "I am so busy and stressed out, I don't have time for a complicated relationship."

Why do teens feel that any committed relationship is automatically complicated? It might seem easier to satisfy the need for an intimate connection with another through physical means—uncommitted sexual encounters. High rates of divorce may imply that commitment is too hard and a breakup is inevitable. Dating apps show so many options, making teens feel like maybe they should wait and keep looking to see if something is better out there.

Hookups—sex without emotional connection—can cause a need to disown parts of ourselves or emotionally detach in an effort to suppress feelings. This strategy can backfire and complicate genuine relationships down the road. It also compromises our ability to trust intimacy. Something so intimate often brings up emotions, whether we want it to or not.

Communication with your teen is key when it comes to sexual exploration. It can be hard to broach the subject of sex with your teen. However, the saying "It is better to hear it from their parents than their friends" applies here. Today it is more than a few friends who are talking to them about sex. They may be exposed to a barrage of information online, much of which is not age appropriate. Hearing from a parent is crucial.

We all have different morals, values, and ideals around sex. It is important for parents not only to share theirs but to listen to their teens. Find out how your teen feels about sex and what ideals they have begun to develop. Just telling them what to do will most likely backfire. Hear them out about the pressures they are facing. Talk to them about what consensual sex looks like, including if someone is negotiating sex with them. Are they just trying to please the other person, or is it something they really want to do? Share how we can all get swept away in the moment and how substances can influence our choice to engage in physical intimacy. Encourage them to discuss with friends how they can keep one another safe if substances are involved.

Again, it is not you just telling them but allowing their expression of opinion and asking questions. Your teens will develop their own values with you helping them along the process as opposed to just taking yours on. This back-and-forth open conversation brings safety and closeness. The CDC reports that "most teens say they share their parents' values about sex, and making decisions about delaying sex would be easier if they could talk openly and honestly with their parents."[11]

Parents need to show a genuine interest in teens' relationships because of the emotional impact. Unfortunately, technology today hinders teens from moving on after a romantic breakup. They have never been easy, but breakups now last longer, with more agonizing pain. Teens tell me their curiosity gets the best of them, and they can't help but stalk their ex. Peering into their whereabouts and wondering who they are with quickly becomes an anxiety-provoking analysis: "Does my ex like this person?" "Are they hooking up?" "Have they already forgotten about me?" "Are they already over me?" "Did our relationship mean anything to them?"

Social media provides a way for hurt, broken-up teens to play vengeful games to make the other jealous. "Breadcrumbing" the ex means reaching out every so often to create confusion and keep the other person in limbo. Abundant rumors and gossip online simply add more drama. This is all too much for a young person to navigate and frankly painful for anyone to endure.

News of Catastrophe and Doom, 24/7

Gradually, news access has shifted into a 24/7 cycle of breaking and urgent information. In the past, the news was only offered at specific times of the day. Now a constant barrage of news and information creates a perpetual feeling of chaos in the background. Toxic news brings negative feelings, yet some aren't even aware of the toll it can take on our mental health. News feeds today are all doom and gloom, presenting no certainty or hope that things could get better.

Parents are always trying to scan what needs to be done. The news gives us the same feeling, that there is always a problem to be solved . . . yet the news shares many large-scale disasters where you don't have any control to change the outcome. This can leave everyone feeling helpless.

It's Okay to Avoid the News for a While

I remember as a child knowing it was time to leave the room when my parents or grandparents turned on the news. I didn't like the way hearing the news made me feel. It wasn't something I could describe or have words for at the time.

At age thirty-six, I took a long break from the news. Looking back now and putting words to my feelings, I felt like I was watching a horror movie between intermittent laughing and smiles from news anchors and commercials. I was particularly sensitive to the real-life horrors shown at the time because I had too much stress in my life. Something had to change. So I jettisoned the news for a while, and my psyche felt much better for it.

When the Twin Towers of the World Trade Center were hit on September 11, 2001, news channels initially showed the event on repeat. Over and over, we saw the planes flying into the Twin Towers. Finally, mental health professionals spoke up about how harmful this could be for individuals to repeatedly witness. The news stations agreed to stop airing the images as often.

The 24/7 broadcast of news will continue, but we do have the choice of curating our news feed, checking in less, or turning it off for a while. We can't control the news, but we can support one another to monitor what we let in and when.

News can be a source of confusion for teens. Hearing multiple versions of the same story leaves teens (and all of us) not knowing what to believe and what is actually true. Teens are exposed to various media outlets reporting on politics, one-sided debates, world conflict, and war (to name a few). It seems we are setting an example for our teens that when we disagree, there is a slim chance of working things out in a healthy manner. Having a different viewpoint will result in dirty fighting, treating others as the enemy, and even war. Many people can't discuss certain topics at all for fear of disagreement and conflict. The online world is offering teens a limited view of how to honor another's point of view while maintaining their own. For our teens, 24/7 news is simply too much to handle.

Always on, Never Present: Where Is True Connection with Others?

Commonly, parents have difficulty understanding the differences from when they were a teen to the present day. They relate to their teen by making statements like "It's not that hard. I was a teenager once too." Things are different now.

From my perspective, our "always on" media environment presents a constant interruption to living our daily lives. It bars us from being present with one another and threatens relationship connections. On balance, it does more harm than good to be constantly "connected" to screens and social media and disconnected from those around us.

Screen Time Provides a False Sense of Belonging

Screens and social media tap into some of our most basic needs, like connection and belonging. They serve as escapism, a way to satisfy boredom, and they give us an instant dopamine hit that is hard to replicate.

Whether teens know the people they are connecting with and following or not, the people shown on screen can appear to fulfill the need for belonging. Teens can identify with characters in a show or an influencer on social media. They may feel that the person on-screen is talking directly to them; they feel included in, or a part of, someone else's life. It is too easy to consider the people on screen friends.

- Mia: "I feel like I am a part of a group watching videos, like it's my social world, even though I don't know any of the people I'm following."

Pressure to show up online to be part of a group also exists.

- Izzie: "I didn't have a good social experience in middle school. I had no friends. Now I'm in high school and have found some friends. It feels so good. I'm afraid if I miss a Snapchat, they will drop me from the group."

Escapism Is Natural but Can Become an Unhealthy Habit

We all need a time-out. Escapism can feel like a little break from the reality of daily stress. As with most things, balance is key. After a hard day at school or work, we may want or need to take a bit of time to check out and not think or do anything. That's fine. However, our curiosity can get the best of us. It can take over and prevent moderation of use. Teens share things like "I just meant to go on for a bit, and it turned into two hours. The time flew by." Everyone can relate to that.

- Beth: "I am so exhausted from a long day at school and my demanding soccer schedule that I jump on my phone to check out."

When home life is stressful, teens can turn to screens to withdraw and avoid. They may have little choice in leaving the environment, and screens are a way to escape.

- John: "I figured out that I could put on my gaming headphones and not hear my parents yell at each other. It just feels better to close off in the basement by myself."

We Live in a World of Distractions That Prevent Connection

Many previous simple, day-to-day interactions are now absent from family life. Instead of forming family bonds during downtime, we reach for a distraction.

- Max: "Screens are just what we all do at night."

Today, it is common to get up from a twenty-minute dinner to see everyone instantly reach for their smartphones. This disconnects everyone at the table by redirecting their attention to people—friends and strangers—who aren't even in our presence.

Watching a movie with the family has turned into everyone double screening. That's really not "together time." The attention isn't on each other—cuddling, sharing popcorn, and talking about our shared experience of the movie. Any breaks in entertainment lead to grabbing a phone to check someone's story or the latest notification instead of turning toward each other and talking.

In the past, teens' friends visited and then left so family members could share family time. Now friends never leave. They are always available online or through asynchronous communication.

- Paige: "I don't want to miss out, so I am on social with my friends a lot of the night. I know I have FOMO [fear of missing out]."

A constant pull drags teens and adults alike into separate online worlds that jeopardize true, in-person connection at home.

Missing the Benefits of Boredom

Since turning to screens has become the default during silence or downtime, there is no room for healthy boredom. Whether at home, at the doctor's office, or at a restaurant, screens present a barrier to connection, representing lost opportunities to interact.

Boredom brings not only the opportunity to generate creative thinking, initiating innovative ideas and novelty, but also a valuable connection that fosters endless expansion for building parents' relationship with their teen and guiding their personal growth journey.

Not allowing ourselves to sit and be bored can turn into a need for constant stimulation. We no longer know how to relax, and for the most part, kids have lost unstructured play that is vital to their development.

Using Imagination in the Mountains

My family was recently in the car for many hours on a cattle drive. (Yes, really—a cattle drive!) Of course, driving into the mountains, we lost cell service.

So we had to use our imaginations to entertain ourselves. We brainstormed what we would do if we won the lottery. We discussed our wishes for how to spend the summertime. We played games like Would You Rather?, Name That Artist, and even Twenty Questions. As we tested each other with downloaded music clips and came up with increasingly crazy questions, we laughed and created lasting memories together.

Without boredom, we wouldn't have used our creativity in figuring out how to connect with each other.

Self-Regulation Has to Be Learned

Several studies on young children who were given a screen to soothe or avoid a tantrum showed this inhibited their ability to self-regulate their emotions.[12] Self-regulation has to be learned through practice in both experiences and relationships. Ideally, a parent's reassuring presence helps calm a child's emotional intensity and helps teens learn to calm themselves.

Screens may bring a short-term break at the moment, but in the long run, this can be a detrimental distraction. Screens potentially give teens a way out from dealing with current problems, stress, and relationship strife. Turning to screens teaches them to escape, avoid, and disconnect from the current situation. There is a loss of learning how to sit with uncomfortable feelings, self-reflect, and move through difficult emotions. When we pacify kids with screens, it may reduce immediate discomfort, but no other learning takes place. We must help our children implement healthier coping strategies than numbing out with screens.

As we all know, not dealing with issues or difficult feelings results in being overwhelmed with them at some point. It also creates a pattern of avoidance, shutting down when things get tough. Being able to recognize, tolerate, and move through different emotional states is a life skill of emotional flexibility. Because our teens are run largely by their emotions (amygdala), they need practice through experiences and in their relationship with you—their primary model in regulating. With less interaction due to screens, they are getting less practice. When a live interaction isn't headed in a positive direction, it's a time to learn how to work through difficult moments with each other, like arguments and having differences of opinion. We all know that relationships can get tough and that checking out and shutting down will cause disruption in any relationship.

Only in recent years—starting in the 1990s—has our culture begun to focus on developing emotional intelligence (EQ). Parents must learn and teach how to sense nuances of communication: nonverbals, paraverbals, and reading people's social cues. Teens today often treat their phones as their best friends. It has become their companion from the moment they wake up until they fall asleep. They develop one-way relationships with their phones rather than developing truly sensitive human interactions.

With all the added stress and pressures that screens and social media bring, it can be hard to understand why our teens (or any of us) can't turn them off. Phones and screens are a pervasive part of modern life. Heightening our awareness and consciousness of their effects will help us live with them.

Parents may be trying their best to limit use, but they face an uphill battle. Smartphones can represent so many things to a teen—humor, games, connection to peers, entertainment, and avoidance of issues.

Satisfying these needs, coupled with our natural tendency to be curious, can create an addictive pattern. It's like trying to quit smoking while carrying a pack of cigarettes around in your pocket.

I'll hear from parents statements like "I try to take the phone away from her, but she screams at me. Lately, she has resorted to becoming aggressive. I'm afraid to take the phone away or put any type of parameters on her use of it. So I don't even bring up the subject anymore."

Parents might see what looks like a teen's self-centeredness or rebellion but might actually be digital addiction (DA). Teens follow classic addictive patterns, with the added circumstance that their brains are still developing. As with any addiction, coexisting conditions are common. You may see disrupted sleep patterns, stress, ADHD, depression, and anxiety. It is important to understand one may precede the other and become a vicious cycle. For example, excessive phone use can cause anxiety and/or depressive symptoms, and the conditions of depression and anxiety may result in excessive phone use. In either scenario, a teen's mental health can be compromised.

Peers and the Second Family

Parenting concerns have always included the questions "Who is my teen hanging out with?" and "Is that person a good influence?" These concerns are valid. Teens' need to belong coupled with their impulsivity and inability to think ahead to consequences can cause them to go along with whatever their peers are doing.

Knowing who your teen is hanging out with has gotten more difficult. Schools have gotten larger. Their connections through social media are hard to track. Kids may have fewer face-to-face interactions during summer and after-school hours. Now that we text, it's rare for anyone to come to the door to pick up a date.

A teen's peer group is like a second family to them. *The Second Family* by Ron Taffel and Melinda Blau encourages us to welcome this second family into our lives. They suggest we find ways to incorporate our teens' friends into our lives as much as we can by inviting them to meals, vacations, concerts, and more. Create space in your home where kids can come hang out. Food always works well to encourage camaraderie! Give your teen's peers respect and the benefit of the doubt. Just as kids are less likely to break the rules when they feel connected with their parents, their friends might also "think twice" once they get to know you.[13]

Setting Healthy Standards for Your Family

So what are parents to do when trying to raise a child amid this backdrop of chaos? You don't want to mess things up, but you don't have full control over what your teen might be exposed to daily. One solution is to lead by example.

Unfortunately, parents can tend to be just as bad or worse than their teens when it comes to screen time. Teens say it doesn't make sense why they should have limited screen time while their parents are scrolling feeds or binge-streaming shows. I hear the word *hypocrite* often.

Even if parents are working (nine to five and beyond), teens see them on a screen, at home but not present. Distracted and disconnected from home life.

Remember, teens are more likely to listen if parents model behaviors they want to see. A cultural shift is needed in homes—for all members of the family, not just singling out kids and teens.

When it comes to phones, ideally, we're setting reasonable limits when we initially give them a phone. It's a gradual process. We don't give our teens the car keys and let them head out on the highway. We get in the car with them and start in parking lots and side streets. We also don't send our kids to R-rated movies. We start with G-rated family fare. I am a huge fan of watches or flip phones initially. At minimum, wait until the beginning of high school for smartphones. Internet-connected activities, including social media, can be seen as an interstate highway. Teens need assistance navigating it. Delaying and minimizing use is what's most beneficial for teens' mental health.

The best practice is usually working with your teen to set limits. Ask them about healthy boundaries for where they are headed online and for how long. Teens may not know what is appropriate or not, and their curiosity can get the best of them. Teens do know that four hours per day is too much time online; you don't need to tell them that. Most teens seem shocked when they really look at their use, and they do want to make changes. They just can't see how it is possible unless compelling alternatives exist.

Teens' technology use can become a dialogue of discovery. Rather than telling them not to use tech, explore with your teen their reasons for wanting to be online and share possible downfalls that come with use.

Ask your teen questions along these lines:

- Who do you enjoy following online?
- How do your thoughts, feelings, or moods vary depending on who you follow?
- How does your screen and social media use affect how you view yourself?
- Do you use the phone to escape anything that is going on, such as hard times at school, social situations, conflicts with friends, or even things going on at home?

- Do you think your phone use increases when you feel stressed, anxious, or down? (Do you know that most likely an increase in use will increase painful feelings?)

Takeaway: Emotional Connections within the Family Must Take Top Priority Today

Screens create separateness and disconnection. Too often, families are looking down at screens instead of looking at each other. Parents and teens may have difficulty forming emotional connections without making eye contact. Surgeon General Dr. Vivek Murthy noted, "You can feel lonely even if you have a lot of people around you because loneliness is about the quality of your connections."[14]

At any given moment, your teen's nervous system may be hyperactivated. Beyond the normal teenage changes and transitions and any family strife, they are dealing with high-pressure scenarios at school and in extracurriculars. The 24/7 news cycle delivers constant doom and gloom. Plus, they face a constant barrage of input over social media, images prompting comparison, and behaviors instilling fear of rejection by their peers.

Using devices is not only about boundaries; it is also about giving teens alternatives to screen use. The alternatives must include genuinely connecting with *you* daily.

Chapter 2 discussed ways to spend quality time and cultivate closeness. It takes effort to plan quality time and creativity to find activities you can do together. However, the effort is necessary to help our teens choose a life of true connectedness. Model to them how you choose to connect with them. That way, they ultimately can choose quality time with you and other people over easy yet less fulfilling connections with their phones.

The next chapter briefly reviews how adult relationships and divorce impact a teen.

Chapter 7 Reflection: Check Disrupted Connections

- Am I considering my own screen use at home?

- Are we as a family scheduling a specific time away from screens and connecting through activities together?

- Am I considering my exposure to news and social media and their impact on my thoughts, feelings, and mood?

- Am I using technology to create a sense of family belonging—for example, a family group text sending kind, encouraging, good-luck, "thinking-of-you" messages? Or is technology being used as a way to only share to-dos and argue?

- How am I redirecting screen time? (Instead of saying, "Get off your device!" consider asking thought-provoking questions like "Have you had in-person time with your friends today?" "Have you moved your body today?" or "Can we have some time together?")

- Is my teen's mental health compromised by the pressures of academics, extra-curriculars, and social media?

CHAPTER 8

Modeling Healthy Adult Relationships

Parents Provide the Main Relational Model

Parent-to-parent interactions set the tone for feelings of connectedness at home. All people initially develop their relationship skills by "learning through observation." Most relational partners mimic what their own parents modeled unless they have done the work to make conscious shifts. Therefore, relationships are tricky; they can inevitably carry baggage from one's own childhood.

Shedding Light on Common Situations

The following is a look at marriage, divorce, stepparenting, and blending of families through the lens of promoting connectedness. If your marriage or relationship with a significant other contains conflict or you have been divorced, please know that the intent of this section is not to cast blame but rather to shed light on situations and circumstances that might affect teens' sense of secure attachment, belonging, and connectedness with each parent.

How you are with your teen impacts them for a lifetime, and how you conduct yourself with your teen's other parent (stepparent, significant other) not only makes an impression on their immediate life but greatly affects their outlook and competencies well into adulthood. How parents handle conflict shapes everything from the child's future ability to accept love and intimacy in relationships to their own self-esteem in any endeavor.

A teen's observational learning through the marital relationship (parent to parent) ideally demonstrates a model of connectedness that reinforces emotional safety in the home. Teens benefit from seeing a loving dyad, where each parent cares for and supports each other, working through difficulties in a healthy way. The relationship shows that trust between two people creates freedom from criticism and contempt, exuding warmth and ease as they relate to each other.

Marital conflict is common and inevitable. However, prolonged discord between parents becomes stressful for everyone at home. Ongoing parental conflict creates a climate of instability, bringing a loss of security. Teens say it feels chaotic at home when parents argue. They often feel angry that they have to deal with parental conflict. Teens can think, "My parents are the adults, and they are supposed to keep me safe, but somehow this doesn't feel safe."

Researchers note that "marital conflict can cause family life to be emotionally unpleasant, threaten the child's emotional or even physical well-being, result in a breakdown of discipline practices, and reduce the emotional availability or sensitivity of parents."[1]

How parents treat each other impacts a child's connection with both parents. Conflict between parents may cause a lack of the child's respect for one or both parents. For example, when one parent is critical of the other, a teen may see a glimmer of truth in the comment and develop a lack of respect or start to reject the parent. On the flip side, a teen may see the critical parent as the one who is behaving unkindly. This can spark anger at or disrespect for that parent. Either way, conflict can compromise a teen's ability to feel connected with any parental figure—parent(s) or stepparent(s).

Parental conflict can cause damage to children whether parents are together or living in separate homes. Conflict is what is harmful. When a teen becomes the subject of an argument, it can bring them additional layers of difficult feelings. They may feel at fault or guilty about their parents' discord. When your parenting styles differ and you argue in front of your teen, it can be confusing. They may end up feeling like they have to take sides. Being on the same page about parenting is not your teen's responsibility. It is best to discuss parenting issues and reach agreements without your teen present.

To help avoid conflict, parents should discuss (ideally before the kids are born) each person's parenting philosophy and the overall values/morals each wishes to instill in their child. Then the couple can discuss how each individual sees common ideals being executed daily. This can help parents get on the same page when it comes to disciplining their kids and day-to-day interactions. Often, parents argue about the small stuff, but in actuality, they agree on the big picture. When looking at the high-level viewpoint, seeing you agree may make it easier to be less rigid with the small stuff.

Parents show their teens how to move through disagreements, how to honor a differing opinion, and whether it is safe to be in a close relationship. The parent-to-parent (or stepparent/partner) dyad provides lessons for your teen and a model for relationships that they will most likely follow.

Divorce: How to Deal with the Stress and Shifts Required

The marriage rate and the divorce rate both declined in the last decade or so (according to census data from 2011 to 2021).[2] Although the divorce rate has hit a fifty-year low, divorce is still quite common today.[3]

Unfortunately, ending a marriage is painful for all involved. Divorce brings stress to the whole family. Parents breaking up requires emotional adjustments in addition to the many practical changes brought to teens' daily lives.

Togetherness as a family will look and feel different. Holidays, summers, birthdays, and teens' sporting events or performances all have a noticeably different feel when parents aren't attending together.

Teens will likely be splitting their time between two parents, living in two different homes. Circumstances of divorce can threaten their sense of safety. Consciously or unconsciously, the question "Will my needs be met while at either home?" arises for children.

Teens grapple with seeing each of their major attachment figures for less time. They experience many feelings due to lack of contact with each parent. They say things like "I miss my mom when I am with my dad and miss my dad when I am with my mom. I feel guilty for having fun with either of them because I think the other is sad and lonely."

The new schedule, whether structured or not, can be hard. The goal is to balance time with each parent while still giving teens some sense of freedom and autonomy in their own lives. Teenagers and parents can feel caught up in the struggle to find enough time. When returning from one parent's home to another, parents may want to spend one-on-one time, while teens may prefer to make plans with friends. Continually cultivating the parent-teen relationship can be a challenge.

When changing homes, missing something they need (want) at the other house can cause stress. They may think, "I am tired of lugging my stuff back and forth. I just want to stay in one house." Teens can become stressed by thoughts of wanting to make it simple and live in one house while dealing with the idea of missing the other parent if they make that choice.

Adjusting to the newness of a separation is taxing and can cause the energy in both homes to feel drained. Different rules at each house can make living conditions confusing and stressful for kids. Teens may want to "work the system," requesting to stay at one house more often than another. This may evoke guilt, as getting what they want in the short term costs them time with one parent over the other.

Parents may have been thinking about divorce for a while before the decision was final. They may have processed their feelings and even moved on by the time they tell their teen. This puts the parent and teen in differing stages of the grieving process of the separation.

Teens need time and space to process their feelings about their parents not being a couple any longer, all the changes to their daily lives, and what this means for the longer term. Kids are in a vulnerable position. They lose time with each parent, which may impact their attachment to both parents.

Parents being further along in processing the divorce may bring in romantic interests before a teen has the chance to process their parents' separation. To a teen, this can feel a bit like piling on to an already difficult situation they are trying to manage.

Because parents may be further along in processing the divorce, they may not show sadness or grief about the marriage dissolving. This can impact a teen and their ability to process their own feelings. They may feel the need to hide their feelings if they sense no one else is having a hard time. They may think, "Is it just me? Why am I sad but my parents don't seem sad?" or "We talked about it once and then never again."

Check in regularly. Invite open communication. Create safety by allowing teens to express their feelings about the separation. Parents do this by being understanding and empathetic—just being there to listen to your teen matters. Acknowledge that the transition is hard. Don't minimize their feelings or the impact it has on them day to day. Parents can express their sadness about the dissolution of the marriage. However, teens' feelings need to be at the center of the discussion.

Monica: Still Processing Her Parents' Divorce at Age Forty-Three

Monica and her husband came in for couples therapy. During our work, Monica expressed her feelings about her parents' divorce, which was finalized twenty-seven years ago. She was still experiencing fallout, emotionally and practically, in juggling seeing both parents on holidays and special occasions.

Monica described the need to bury her feelings about her parents' divorce when she was a teen. She said, "If I shared how I was feeling, I had to hear someone's side of the story. Their perspective was filled with negative comments and feelings toward my other parent. So I pretended I was fine."

She added, "Eventually, I worked myself into being fine. I have tried to bury it for so long, I am surprised it is bubbling up now."

When Divorce Is Contentious

Involving kids in divorce, conflict, picking sides, bad-mouthing, and financial decisions is never okay. Research indicates teens' adjustment to divorce is greatly impacted by how well parents get along and work together to co-parent.[4] There are many reasons for parents divorcing. Likely there are unkind words spoken and hurt feelings, and there may even have been infidelity. However, that is between parents. Teens should not be put in the middle of a divorce or an outlet for controlling pain.

Often when someone is hurting, they feel out of control internally, and controlling things externally makes one think they will feel better. Teens often become the pawns in a punishing game with the ex. Being put in the middle causes stress and confusion to a teen, even if unintentional. This can have a lasting negative impact on a teen's own mental health.

When a parent bashes the other parent, it is telling a teen two things: (1) the teen shouldn't love the other parent for some reason, and (2) parts of them aren't loveable.

Teens see themselves in both parents. When a parent points out something is wrong with the other parent, a teen can think, "I am kind of like Mom/Dad. Does that mean that part sucks about me too? Does that mean Mom/Dad doesn't like that about me?"

If your teen is having trouble in their relationship with their other parent, listen, empathize, and validate their feelings. You can say, "I hear this is hard for you." "I understand you feel . . ." "I am here to listen." Chiming in with details of your relationship with the other parent moves the focus from listening and comforting your teen to you. Finding a therapist for your teen may be necessary to help them navigate the relationship with their other parent.

George: Caught between His Parents in Their Prolonged Divorce

George came to me when he was fourteen and his parents were getting a divorce. They had been in proceedings for one year already, and it didn't look like it would be finalized anytime soon.

George was stressed out dealing with the ever-changing schedule and serving as the go-between for his parents. He would hear about the costs of extracurricular activities, clothes, and incidentals. He was told frequently to ask the other parent for money. He passed checks back and forth. He was the messenger, forced to deal with the fallout from each parent when the message wasn't something they wanted to hear.

There was talk about court proceedings, and he even had one parent ask him to read court documents. One comment he made that has always stuck with me was "I don't understand how two people who were once seemingly in love, dancing in the living room, now hate each other."

Having your child's best interest at heart means keeping the details of a divorce and negative feelings about the other parent to yourself—*no matter your child's age.*

Beyond Contentious: Parental Alienation Syndrome

The APA defines parental alienation syndrome (PAS) as "a child's experience of being manipulated by one parent to turn against the other (targeted) parent and resist contact with them. This alignment with one parent and rejection of the other most often arises during child custody disputes following divorce or separation."[5]

Parental alienation syndrome goes beyond talking negatively about the other parent (whether together or divorced). One parent encourages the child or teen to treat the targeted parent with disrespect or hostility. It is behavior that creates hatred for the other parent. A loss of contact with the targeted parent most likely extends to other relatives of the targeted family. PAS is dangerous and comes with a psychological cost to teens.

It is common for a parent who alienates to be dealing with mental health issues. The best thing a targeted parent can do for their children is seek professional help. Getting a second opinion from a well-regarded subject matter expert can ensure one's view of an ex's behavior isn't tainted by the relationship. This can help protect your teen. Prioritize the goal of keeping children and teens physically and psychologically safe.

Integrating a New Partner or Stepparent

When a parent finds someone new and falls "head over heels," be aware that teens may not be experiencing all the same "good feels" as the new couple. Bringing someone new into the family circle needs to be done with well-thought-out intention. Ideally, before making introductions between the new partner and the children, ensure this is an established relationship. Six to twelve months can allow for the infatuation phase to settle down. Waiting can help you see more clearly through euphoria (a normal biological reaction your body produces early in courtship). People can't stay on their best behavior for too long. Daters will start to see more of the person and less of the attraction with time. A teen's ability to build trust with a new person will likely be easier when they know you have taken care and time doing your own due diligence.

Time a couple spends together cultivating the new relationship may vastly differ from the teen's time spent with the new partner. Adults may have spent much more time learning about each other, getting comfortable in the relationship, and bonding. Parents need to be cognizant of this so they don't rush the teen to "like" their new partner. Connection can't be forced.

Being attuned to your teen's comfort level with your new partner is important. Let your teen lead the process. The parent can ask their teen how they feel about someone new in their life. If it is too close to the time of separation, a teen may not feel ready. A parent listening, empathizing, and validating their teens' feelings about someone new being around them will help the teen process the new situation.

Much care needs to be taken to prepare for major transitions, such as when the relationship evolves to a partner living in the same home or to a new marriage. Honor that it may be difficult for a teen to form a new family structure. With a stepparent coming into the family circle, a teen may unconsciously or consciously revisit the fact that their parents aren't getting back together, bringing up hurt feelings and challenging behaviors.

For stepparents making the transition, open communication works best. A stepparent might say, "I am not here to replace your mom/dad. Let's figure out together how to define my role in your life." Start with gaining mutual respect and the mindset of growing the friendship first. Let the teen know you are there to support them in any way they would like your support. Assure the teen that you won't be taking away time they spend with either of their parents. You will still honor their own one-on-one time.

Stepparents need to evoke the lessons of cultivating belonging and connection, too, finding shared interests, initiating greetings, and being a part of daily family connecting times like dinner. They can offer to help with homework or drive a teen to school or extracurriculars. Provide daily contact and casual get-to-know-you chats to build the relationship in nonthreatening ways. It is important that stepparents speak up when they see a teen's accomplishments, share encouraging words, and point out the positive qualities of their new stepchild. Teens always benefit when an adult shows them genuine interest and positive reinforcement.

Stepparents will need to be patient. It may take time for a teen to get used to a new person living in the same space and sharing a bedroom with a parent (one of the teen's primary attachment figures).

Not Feeling Welcomed at Home

Claire had struggled with her mother meeting someone new. Seven years after her mother married her stepfather, she chose to write her college essay about the impact he had on her life. The following is an excerpt from her essay:

When my mom introduced me to her friend, Nick, I could tell by the way she laughed at his jokes that he was more than a friend. She wanted to know what I thought about him. I would shrug and look aloof. Deep down, I felt defensive about Nick from the day he entered our lives, thinking all men were like my dad.

Nick often ate dinner with us and would even come to watch my soccer games. He made every effort to be friendly. One day, I said something that pushed Nick's buttons and realized that he wasn't just upset; he was sad. He told me, "I want you to respect me the way I respect you. I really want to make this work." I wanted to be respectful, but my urge to protect my mother caused me to say hurtful things and give him dirty looks, so he felt unwelcome.

That day was a turning point in our relationship. When Nick showed me his true feelings, his sadness allowed me to let down my protective walls. I began to trust him and trust that we all could be happy together.

Nick showed me that a relationship can be positive but that even a good relationship will experience ups and downs. When occasional arguments arose, we were respectful, honest, and patient. Nick taught me forgiveness, trust, and commitment. I proudly spoke at their wedding, welcoming Nick into our family. I felt blessed to have a loving father (stepfather) who is involved in my life. I love Nick and feel happiest when he introduces me as his daughter.

Instead of teens getting in trouble for giving their stepparent the cold shoulder, sit down and talk with them about what's going on. It hurts to be in a negative place with your stepchild. That could make anyone angry. However, sharing the feelings underneath will result in a better outcome; your feelings show your human side. Your stepchild likely knows what it feels like to be dismissed and/or rejected. This allows empathy to grow.

Blending families can be complicated. When there are more members to blend, the more complicated it can get. More people means more personalities and multiple dynamics. Open dialogue is key: take the time to discuss how the relationships are feeling, and utilize the volley during conversations and conflict. It is okay to still have time with your own kids individually, but always create times when you are together as a family unit. Discuss as a family unit traditions old and new that you would like to experience together. These will serve as bonding moments and create a foundation for your new family unit. In time, the integrated family time will feel more natural and cohesive.

Just as biological parents have discovery conversations about parenting philosophies, these same conversations need to happen with someone who will become a stepparent. This doesn't mean the stepparent is "parenting" or delivering consequences; alignment on parenting ideals cuts down on frustrations and conflict between adults. It is best in the beginning for a stepparent to ease into the role and cultivate a friendship first. When stepparents immediately jump into the role of decision-maker for teens, it can backfire. Often teens express, "He/she just came into my life. I don't really know them, and now they are telling me what to do."

If previously agreed-upon boundaries or house rules exist, teens know their stepparent isn't trying to rule the roost. They are just following through with what their parent has already put in place.

A stepparent has a unique role. They are coming into the relationship with a fresh eye. They may see a parent's blind spots (which everyone has) concerning their teen. They may voice them, and this can feel threatening to the biological parent and cause conflict. It can be hard to see and then own up to our blind spots. Parents may react by defending themselves and their teen instead of taking ownership. If values and parenting philosophies are aligned with your new spouse, it can be helpful insight. Use your partner as a sounding board and allow for open dialogue. This also gives the stepparent a voice without directly disciplining.

Stepparenting another child may be hard, but it is an opportunity to make a positive impact on a teen's life. A stepparent can be one more respected figure in a teen's life who shows interest in them, recognizes their accomplishments, and lets them know how special and important they are. With such support, a stepparent can give a teen the sense that another person has their back. Stepparenting provides the opportunity for a teen to feel care and love from one more person.

Takeaway: What Parents Model in Their Adult Relationships Greatly Impacts Their Teen

Whether you're married, separated, or divorced or have never married, every parent and significant other can strive to create stronger relational bonds. Teens benefit from a healthy, emotionally well-regulated relational model. Because teens see themselves in both parents, it's important to help them build a healthy relationship with each parent.

Parental conflict stresses children out and can cause mental hardship whether parents are together or living in separate homes. If there is contentiousness or discord, seek help for yourself and your kids. Let the chain of conflict stop with you.

Reflect on your relationship with your significant other. Use the interactional model (described in chapter 6). The dynamic is a bit different between two adults with long histories (perhaps the subject of the next book!), but much discussed here applies. This book was intended as a journey for you as a parent of a teen. However, having your spouse/partner read the book and answer the self-reflection questions will help ensure you are both speaking the language of connectedness.

The next chapter emphasizes normalizing the sharing of feelings at home.

Chapter 8 Reflection: What Are You Modeling?

- Is your relationship with your spouse or significant other modeling connectedness?
- Do you and your spouse (or partner or ex) have similar philosophies on parenting?
- Do your actions show your children how to resolve conflict in a healthy manner?

When Divorced

Ask yourself,

- How is the hurt from my divorce coming through in my interactions with my kids?

- What messaging am I sending to my kids about the other parent?
- Am I involving them in the divorce proceedings?
- Am I trying to get back at my ex through my kids?
- Are they stuck in the middle?
- Am I adultifying my children by involving them in my issues with the divorce?
- Am I treating them as my confidant?

On the Flip Side

Ask yourself,

- Am I working through the difficult process of divorce with my teen's other parent?
- Are we co-parenting together?
- Are we making sure we are still facilitating a sense of belonging with each parent in both homes?
- Are we encouraging a secure connection with both parents?
- Are we getting help if we are having difficulty getting along and co-parenting to alleviate stress for our teen?

CHAPTER 9

Transparency and Connectedness, a Positive Feedback Loop

The Path Forward: Normalizing Talking about Feelings at Home

An essential part of creating a healthy relational world is emotional openness about thoughts and feelings, both positive and negative. Clearly expressing how we feel, our desires, and our needs with those close to us increases connectedness. Personal expression impacts our happiness and the success of our relationships.

When asking teens and parents if their relationship is close, their answers often diverge. Closeness means different things to teens and parents. The perceived level of closeness for teens today depends on openness and reciprocal sharing of feelings. For many parents, discussions and openness about feelings aren't something that happened in their family of origin. We know a lot more about the role emotions play in our lives than we did even twenty years ago.

We know that sharing positive feelings with those close to us who reciprocate our reach brings closeness to the relationship. Hearing from and being able to say to those close to you "I appreciate you," "I love you," or "I enjoy spending time with you" bring feelings of internal warmth. Sharing positive feelings both verbally and nonverbally releases oxytocin (the hormone of attachment).

We also know that hiding and burying our less pleasant feelings doesn't always work. Over time, they can catch up to us. We can be left with feelings that build up and drag us down. It can greatly impact our relationships with others. We can cause disconnection by throwing our "emotional mud" at those close to us or by simply checking out of the relationship. Running from our feelings may cause us more problems.

Avoiding feelings can impact both our mental health and how we function daily. In fact, much discussion in recovery groups is about buried feelings and shame that drive the need to numb out. Often, tough feelings were left unattended because it wasn't acceptable to express them and/or the individuals in recovery (and their primary caregivers) didn't know how. It wasn't something they learned growing up.

We know all humans have the same emotions and feelings. We all have a limbic system, so there is a commonality in all of our emotional inner workings. We all have tear ducts that activate when we are sad, overwhelmed, or happy. Underneath anger, a common go-to emotion, lies many other feelings—sadness, frustration, loneliness, stress, shame, and fear. If we all experience the same feelings, why don't we just talk about them? When you think about it, it's kind of odd.

When someone takes the time to really listen, we feel seen and heard. When those closest to us empathize and validate, we feel understood. We have these needs in common no matter our age, race, ethnicity, culture, socioeconomic condition, gender identity, or religious orientation. No one wants to feel they are doing life all by themselves. Support brings relief and the feeling that we aren't alone. Teens want emotional closeness with their parents, and that means normalizing communicating with feelings at home.

Teens need a place where they don't have to conceal any parts of themselves, where they are able to share their innermost thoughts and feelings without hesitation. Yes, teens typically share with friends, but the opportunity to be fully transparent with their friends may not exist. This is especially true if they fear it will result in a rumor or a social media nightmare. Home should be one place where they don't have to hold back.

Vulnerability Is a Stepping-Stone to Emotional Transparency

When thinking about sharing thoughts, feelings, and needs, the word *vulnerability* comes to most minds. We hear from experts, therapists, and even pop culture that we must "feel vulnerable" in order to express our internal world with others. There has been much studied and written on the topic that indicates "being vulnerable" is the key to creating closeness and lasting happiness in relationships.

My experience has taught me something else. *I believe emotional transparency is what creates real, safe, and loving relationships. Shifting the focus from vulnerability to transparency allows for true connectedness at home.*

The reason for this conceptual shift? Vulnerability implies risk. In our family relationships, we should not have to be at risk when sharing how we feel—especially not our children and teens.

In new relationships, you are learning about each other, wondering if you will find acceptance with a new person. It makes sense that one could almost feel constant vulnerability. However, the parent-child relationship isn't new! This relationship should be characterized by safe and open shares, not the feeling that it is a risk (a vulnerability) to share one's truth. No one wants to feel uncertainty at home. Yet this is the reality for many teens.

At times it seems the term *vulnerability* is overused. We can benefit from seeing vulnerability not as the end result of sharing our innermost thoughts and feelings but as a stepping-stone to emotional transparency. Too often these days, we get stuck on the stepping-stone. We need to focus on taking the next step: reaching a state of emotional transparency with our teens.

Vulnerability

Vulnerability has a huge range of definitions, ranging from "being exposed to the possibility of being attacked or harmed"[1] to "uncertainty, risk, and emotional exposure."[2] For our purposes, vulnerability is offering up thoughts and feelings without knowing if there will be acceptance. It is putting yourself in a circumstance where you feel unsure of how a listener will react. The risks of being vulnerable include rejection, feelings of abandonment, judgment, hurt, and shame.

Home needs to be the place that minimizes emotional risk. How you are with your teen tells them whether it is safe to express their internal world with you.

Emotional safety allows for an unfiltered relationship. Sharing fears and insecurities. Reaching out when you aren't doing well emotionally or you've done something not so perfect. Disclosing needs and disappointments about the relationship means transparency. Reaching out for parental emotional support shouldn't feel unsafe, exposing, or shameful or cause worry about a parent's reaction. You don't want a fear of judgment or abandonment to stop your teen from reaching out to you, their primary attachment figure.

Emotional Transparency

Transparency is where you openly share your internal state and invite others to do the same without judgment.

Parents can reduce the emotional risk of family members sharing thoughts, feelings, and needs by listening nonreactively and by sharing their own internal states. Parents build trust through healthy communication, the absence of judgment and fear-based parenting, and feelings of mutual acceptance. Trust and safety enable transparency.

We can't mindread or anticipate what another is thinking, feeling, or needing, including your teen. Being transparent allows us all to understand each other. Much confusion, misunderstandings, and "rebellion" could be avoided if we all expressed what was really going on inside of us. If we volleyed. Parents need to take the lead in volleying with their teens.

The back-and-forth volley, a rhythmic expression of thoughts and feelings, is what moves a relationship from a vulnerable state to a transparent one. Clear self-expression becomes an easy volley between parents and teens once trust has been established. Once you're in the regular rhythm of sharing, you can more easily discuss what's happening within you and between the two of you. With regular practice, talking about thoughts and feelings becomes second nature.

A parent's reassurance allows teens to again feel safe to share. They tend to think, "Yes, this is another topic I can bring to my parents." Teens who share deeper thoughts and feelings with their parents find relief, empowerment, and freedom. There is no reason to hide. Shame and self-questioning disappear. This is how transparency safeguards against feeling emotionally alone in any relationship.

When expressing feelings is a daily practice, it no longer feels so "vulnerable" to open up; it is simply what you do. Eventually, vulnerability takes a back seat and shows up less often. Fewer "big feelings" stop you and your teen from opening up. Each person can relax, sensing, "I don't have to hold any parts of myself back."

To be clear, transparency at home doesn't mean expressing every single feeling or thought exactly when it arises. It means creating an environment at home that allows for safe, open sharing. Parents and teens are both sensitive and compassionate with each other.

Of course, to normalize talking about feelings, parents need to be aware, comfortable, and able to express their own feelings. Parents must be willing and able to handle talking about various and difficult subjects. When parents are comfortable with openness—when they are able to volley—their teens will soon follow. In this way, whatever parents normalize transcends for a lifetime. We need a cultural shift inside our homes to reduce the stigma of talking about feelings. Eventually, this will extend to life outside the home, giving teens more of a chance to have happy, healthy relationships with others.

Throughout this book, you have read the many ways to build trust with your teen. You now know how to make space for a rhythmic volley, sharing openly. When trust is built, safety is established, and the "feelings of vulnerability" subside. It may take time, but you now know how to encourage closeness in the parent-teen relationship.

With the shift of focus from vulnerability to emotional transparency, you can feel free to reveal your inner thoughts, feelings, and needs; you don't have to put up your guard or create walls between yourself and others. You feel secure enough to be open with one another, and that brings a sense of freedom.

The goal is to encourage emotional transparency at home, reduce feelings of vulnerability, and allow emotional transparency to grow.

Noticing Concerns Early and Often
Builds Safety and Transparency

"I have something I want to talk to you about . . . but I'm kind of embarrassed to bring it up."

When my ten-year-old daughter expressed this, I responded with a volley: "I am open to anything you have to ask me." I thought, "Aren't I always open to hearing what you have to say?" but instead of getting defensive and making it about me, I waited patiently and listened.

She described that a classmate had started shaving. My daughter was wondering if it was time to start shaving her legs as well. I responded, "It sounds like this was hard for you to bring up. This is what I am here for, to talk to you about difficult topics and figure out this big transition to becoming a teenager. I totally get why you are asking. I feel like it is a little early to start shaving, but I am happy to hear more about why this is important to you."

Teens will be embarrassed about lots of things! As teens continuously face new situations and challenges, many questions arise. It is all new for them. Undoubtedly, they will feel unsure, even lost, with all they are facing. They need you to be fully present and nonreactive at these times.

They may ask themselves, "Are my parents approachable on this topic? Can I share what I am going through and how I am feeling?" Even when we try our best to be open and listen well, they will still hold back sometimes. The more open we are to continually field any question (without making it about us), the more trust, safety, and transparency we build.

If parents aren't approachable, teens will be left to deal with difficult feelings and tough situations on their own. Working to build trust and a safe emotional environment early (and continually) helps teens feel confident they can come to you with anything as time goes on.

While a preteen asking about shaving legs (as in the story shown) may seem like it's not that big of a deal, it is exactly the kind of moment that demonstrates to kids if it is safe to open up about bigger issues later. If we approach the small, vulnerable moments with a judgment-free and open heart, we create emotional transparency for the long term. These vulnerable moments are the stepping-stones to transparency.

What parents deem as comfortable is likely what teens will be comfortable discussing. Even in the example provided, some level of security already existed, allowing the opening of "I am embarrassed." When teens start a conversation by expressing hesitation, they're being transparent in that moment about their feelings. That indicates it is time for the parent to reassure both themselves and their teen and move the conversation forward. It is a glimmer of vulnerability and a signal to establish safety on a new topic.

Thinking back to the introduction, Ella felt trapped by her feelings in part because she felt she had nowhere to open up. Ella wanted to share her feelings with her mother, yet openly sharing feelings wasn't something they did much at home. So she felt she didn't have a place to go. If your mom didn't talk about challenging topics, then there may be more vulnerability in talking about related subjects. If your dad never said "I love you," you might feel vulnerable expressing your love to someone else. Yet if one or both of your parents did share their struggles and sensitivities with you, those topics would now be on the table for discussion. In the future, within new relationships, these topics may be met with less risk in sharing and a greater ability to be transparent.

The Positive Feedback Loop

Transparency and connectedness exist in a perpetual feedback loop: "The more I can be transparent with you, the more I feel connectedness with you. The more I feel connectedness with you, the more I can be transparent with you."

Being able to be emotionally open brings closeness, and the more you are open, the closer you will feel. Trust and security are cultivated. Deeper feelings can flow. The more the ease of sharing with each other increases, the more you experience an internal warmth that drives your interaction with each other.

This feeling of connectedness deepens the relationship. It breeds feelings of reciprocal care in the relationship. Teens are less likely to be dishonest with you. As one teen expressed, "I am allowed to be open. I can tell the truth and not fear their response, even when I mess up." A teen's ability to be honest about what's really going on for them prevents both of you from prolonged hard feelings.

Listening with Heart Positively Impacts Teens' Mental Health

Emotional transparency positively impacts teens' mental health. The need for transparency in the parent-teen relationship is imperative considering the current milieu. Right now, the rates of depression, anxiety, and suicide among youth are at an all-time high. Twenty percent of high schoolers report consistent feelings of sadness and hopelessness, an increase of 40 percent since 2000.[3] The CDC reports suicide rates among teens and young adults have gone up by 57 percent since 2007.[4] In 2021, 22 percent of high school students seriously considered attempting suicide during the past year.[5]

As we have seen, the pressures today's teens face undoubtedly cause much stress to their developing brains—pressures with academics, outside school activities, college entrance requirements, and the high costs of college. The daily pressures, real or perceived, can be equivalent to feelings of training for the Olympics or preparing for attendance at Harvard. Teens even express having difficulty envisioning how they can make it on their own in the current financial landscape.

Use of social media only compounds these stressors by viewing others' lives with the themes "Everyone has it all together, so why don't I?" and "I am not enough in some way." Considering the developmental ability of a teen to manage all this stress has a significant impact on how teens are doing. Too much pressure can equal the need for perfection or result in "I can't reach the bar, so why try?" The pressure can also lead to what seems to be rebellion but is a result of a need to check out from the stress. All of this can compromise a teen's mental health.

When Darker Thoughts Intrude

There is a long-standing myth that if you say the word *suicide*, you will be giving someone the idea to take their life. This myth has been disproven but is still widely believed. Unfortunately, it is preventing much-needed conversations between teens and parents around the topic of suicide, and the culture at large is influential and now often portrays scenes of self-harm.

Often when teens reach my office, they haven't shared with anyone that they are experiencing intrusive thoughts. Thoughts of self-harm and suicide can be common for many, even teens. These thoughts can be very scary. Teens usually describe an internal battle of wanting to tell their parents but being afraid of burdening their parents or freaking them out. So they hold these thoughts and feelings all by themselves. This only makes the common feelings of being trapped when someone is experiencing thoughts of suicide more pronounced. When I ask them, "Are you having thoughts of self-harm or suicide?" I see an immediate relief. I see their bodies relax, and most even verbalize, "Thank you for asking me." Saying the word for them helps them know it is okay to talk about it.

Suicide is a subject parents need to talk about with their teens. Letting them know they can come to you if they ever experience difficult thoughts can save a teen from carrying painful feelings by themselves. If you sense something is wrong, ask the question, "Are you having thoughts of self-harm or suicide?" You are giving them permission to share what's going on for them.

When any of us are struggling, a common tendency is to hide and isolate, causing us to disconnect from those around us, but what we need most is a safe connection. Being open allows movement away from the action tendency to isolate and toward reaching out. If we can regularly reach out and share what's going on for us, it reduces feelings of crisis that come with troubling thoughts. Share with them, "We can feel trapped by our situation or by our thoughts. It can feel like there isn't a way out. But there is."

It's okay to tell young children, "Sometimes when we are frustrated, disappointed, or overwhelmed, our thoughts can go to bad places. Sometimes there seems to be no reason at all when we have these difficult thoughts. We can just get in a bad mental space. Please come tell me when or if this happens to you. I want to know, and I want to be there to help you deal with these thoughts. If I am unsure of what to do, we can seek help together."

We all know what external isolation feels like. We just had that experience with the COVID-19 lockdowns and fears of subsequent viral mutations. The isolation took a toll on our mental health, and we saw how in-person connection was vital to our well-being. Most of us have experienced at times a similar feeling of "aloneness" in life, even while in a close relationship with another person. That feeling of being alone may come from a lack of emotional closeness, a lack of connectedness. It can feel like an internal isolation. Like being on an emotional island by ourselves. It's the feelings of emotional isolation that can be harmful, not mentioning the word *suicide*. Teens need their parents to ask and listen to what's really going on for them inside. They should not need to pretend to have it all together. None of us do.

Other Considerations for Teen Mental Health

Sometimes people think that those who take their lives are only individuals with mental illness. The fact is, more than half of those who die by suicide do not have a mental health diagnosis at the time of their death.[6] That means mental illness is only one of the risk factors for suicide.

Talking to your teen about their own mental health is imperative. Having these conversations is actually part of taking care of your own mental health. Parents can greatly impact their child's ability to cope with the many stressors they face. That includes talking to your teen about how they are feeling and being open to discussing what they may be struggling with.

It is important to know that "globally, it is estimated that 1 in 7 (14%) 10–19 year-olds experience mental health conditions, yet these remain largely unrecognized and untreated."[7] Early intervention and support can help these individuals. Having open conversations provides a better understanding of what your teen is experiencing.

Talking about how you are feeling is, in part, taking care of your mental health. Allow your kids to be transparent with their feelings. Openness about mental health is the first step toward getting needed treatment. Connectedness is suicide prevention.

Gene and Paula: We Are All in This Together

"I just want them to pick up their dishes!" Paula said. Her husband, Gene, chimed in, "Yeah, and they are on their screens too long." In our first family therapy session, Paula and Gene wanted to establish rules and better screen time boundaries with their two teens, fourteen-year-old Tanner and sixteen-year-old Nina.

As their therapist, I, of course, wanted to discuss how the relationships felt for each of them. I continually asked questions about their relationships with one another. Mom and Dad would inevitably interject about difficulties they were experiencing with one or both of their teens. It was difficult to keep the session on track, discussing the relational component of their family.

Nina had her head down for most of our session, and Tanner didn't say much. Gene called them out: "If you don't participate, there will be a consequence."

I then held individual sessions with each member of the family. During their daughter Nina's individual session, she made continual eye contact and was engaged, and the conversation flowed. About thirty minutes in, I asked Nina what she would like to talk about with her parents and brother in family therapy.

She said she wanted more family time, noting, "We never spend time all together. Mom takes me to do something, and Dad takes my brother somewhere else. We are never all together." Nina wanted the whole family to see her play the violin. She said her brother and her dad never attended her concerts.

Often parents come into family therapy to discuss rules and what a teen isn't doing well. Teens come to therapy wanting to discuss the relationship. I see this dichotomy over and over again in sessions. However, I also see that the closer the relationship, the more likely kids value and respect their parents and the more likely there will be a "pulling together" or "we are in it together" feeling at home. In close relationships, empathy grows for the other. Teens begin to value your opinion, listen, and chip in to help the team.

Why Teens Want to Discuss the Relationship

Teens are looking for a meaningful relationship with their parents. It might be hard to believe, but they are. Parents are the closest people to their kids. It is only natural that kids would want closeness with their parents. They need to feel you aren't just parenting them but that you value your relationship with them and you want closeness.

Most people don't talk about the "relationship," meaning how things are going between each other. Parents may say, "I love you," but a true discussion around how the connection is feeling isn't something many acknowledge. Usually it takes a fight before someone brings up how they are really feeling in the relationship. At that point, they are most likely to bring up their displeasure. It is often shared with volume and stated in extremes, such as "You never . . ." and "You always . . ."

It is quite shocking that we don't often have level-headed discussions with the most important people in our lives about how each person feels in the relationship. When you can discuss the relationship, it can increase closeness. This does require you to hear things about yourself that you may not want to. Keep in mind, all our own perspectives can be mixed with our view of self, misunderstandings, and miscommunication. However, honoring each person's perspective allows each person's experience to matter. This gives you both the opportunity to talk it out, creating clarity, and it can bring you both closer.

Teens need to know you are their mom and dad who value who they are. They want to know that you think highly of them. Teens love to feel that their parents view them in a positive light. They enjoy feeling that they add to your life and that you are happy they are in it with you.

Parents have so much power in their teens' world. Using that power for the positive to build up your teen and let them know you believe in them, you see the possibilities of who they will become that they don't see themselves just yet. Them knowing you see it matters in such a big way. Teens are filled with positive feelings when a parent says, "I am proud of who you are." In fact, that good feeling never stops. Even for adults, hearing from a parent "I am proud of who you are" lands like no other feeling.

Modeling Behavior May Be More Effective Than Rules

Children don't do what you say; they do what you do. Your teen will emulate your behavior. You can lecture all you want, but they will likely follow through with what they see you modeling. In all fairness, you can't expect your kids to do anything differently than you. Whether it's binge-watching TV, yelling, sharing your feelings, saying "I'm sorry," or refraining from incessant smartphone use, it makes sense that your kids will follow your lead.

This can feel like perfection is needed to set an example for your teen. Not the case. What is important is modeling what you want to see from your own teen(s). Think about the values, morals, and behaviors you wish they would cultivate themselves. Then self-reflect on your own behaviors, communication, and habits while asking yourself, If your teen were a mirror image, would that be okay with you? Yes, it can be a challenge.

Each child is different, genetically and in personality. Understanding each child's unique tendencies and preferences means parenting with these distinctions in mind. One of your children may overstudy, while another's tendency is to avoid studying. One may go with the flow, and another may seem rigid. One may have a somewhat addictive nature, and the other may not latch onto anything. Thankfully, parenting can become easier when you start by modeling the standards you want to see (for example, good boundaries for work habits, healthy coping techniques, and getting help when needed). Then you can provide each child the individualized guidance they need to direct them to the standard you exemplify.

Sometimes being present and serving as a good role model can almost feel like rethinking our entire past. Our upbringing results in basically hardwired, unconscious patterns we play out in interactions with others. Some of us have had little training in the language of connectedness. In talk therapy sessions, parents will frequently ask, "Is this how people really talk?"

Yes, people really do talk this way. Tender, connected communication is a skill like any other. And new patterns can emerge and will feel more comfortable with practice.

Secure Attachment Is Co-regulating

Parents are still the most influential people in a teen's life. That means you have an incredible opportunity to make a difference in how your teen handles the stressors they face. Your emotional availability, attunement, and sensitivity will calm their stress.

Beyond those early years, the co-regulating volley has progressed into a rhythmic verbal exchange. A transparent expression of thoughts, feelings, and needs. Communication with feelings. This exchange also encompasses feelings of warmth in both the presence of physical contact and the tone of voice. This is the language of connectedness.

Trust is the major component to allow the volley to occur. Building an environment at home that fosters a sense of belonging is pivotal in teens being able to be soothed by you in times of distress. Unconditional acceptance is building trust to enable this reach. A teen feeling acknowledged, important to you, and welcomed builds security in the relationship.

A teen in distress may exhibit many different signs that may not immediately register with parents as "signals of distress." We tend to notice worry (which could indicate anxiety) or sadness (depression), but teens may appear combative instead. They may show signs of irritability, agitation, and anger—pushing you away—as opposed to saying, "I need you." Trust between you can help remove any defenses so you can more clearly see their state of mind. Have confidence that you will be a force of comfort in these times, enabling them to reach for you more directly.

As a parent, being in tune and recognizing your teen's cues that something is off require you to put aside the assumptions that your teen is just being "a typical teen." Be curious in your communication by asking questions to gain an understanding of their emotional experience. Look at what is behind the behavior. Listen to understand, not to defend. Rather than jumping to problem-solving, jump into their emotional experience. You can be a calming presence with the tone of your voice and the warmth of your physical contact. All of which builds trust so your teen can reach for you when they are anxious, are struggling, or have a need. This brings emotional closeness. It is the emotional closeness that brings calm, comfort, and reassurance to your teen. That is co-regulating.

Research shows that satisfying and secure family relationships are a major predictor of happiness.[8] The effects of growing up with a secure attachment positively impact mental health and physical well-being. Positivity impacts feelings about the self: self-worth and self-esteem. Secure attachment is shown to build resilience and autonomy. Teens will be more in tune with their and others' emotional states. Secure attachment with a parent positively impacts the ability to trust others and form future committed relationships. They will have a greater ability to express feelings and love to another.[9]

The Idea of Emotional Self-Sufficiency Is Bunk

Culture tells us we need to be (and train our kids to be) independent and self-sufficient. However, humans are relational and are meant to rely on one another. Being in relation with one another contributes to having lasting happiness and mental and physical well-being. Being conscious of messages sent to your teen about self-sufficiency matters. Yes, being financially self-sufficient is good! (Yet even this task may be difficult in the present day.) Actually, the idea of emotional self-sufficiency is bunk. Social isolation brings severe mental health consequences.

Attempting to be self-sufficient regarding emotional needs may result in emotional loneliness. Ideas of being self-sufficient impact how and if a teen asks for emotional support. It can impact their ability to identify their emotional needs and feel okay about having them. Teens may think, "I am too much for my parents. I can't ask for comfort when I am stressed, sad, or upset. I have to take care of it myself."

None of us want to feel like we are "too much" for those close to us. We all want to be able to express our feelings and needs in a relationship. Transparency is a big part of what makes healthy relationships. When we can create a safe space for our kids to share how they are feeling, they are open to sharing it all, the good and bad. Them being able to talk about their inner world says, "Your emotions aren't too much for me to handle. Please share with me."

Being able to express how they are feeling also brings their understanding of their own needs. It can be a task trying to find where needs lie both as an individual and within a relationship. Defining our needs is important for both our own mental well-being and the success of our relationships. Teens need the back and forth of volleying with their parents to discover how to reach out to others to get their needs met. They also learn to accept comfort from those close to them. These lessons provide essential cues for all their future relationships.

Simply knowing they can come to you—to express how they feel or talk about struggles—actually helps teens handle their emotions better internally. It also means "I am worthy of your time and love."

Back to the Changing Table

It's been twenty-five years since that first evening staring down at my newborn on the changing table. I have had two more children since that day. I spent many of those early years as a mom worried my children would feel some of the loneliness and suffering that I felt at different times in my own childhood. In an effort to make their lives free from any hurt, I tried to make it perfect. This resulted in me being an anxious mom at the start. With time I realized that my worry for everything to be perfect for them was having the opposite effect. I discovered my often anxious state caused me to be rigid. I was filled with stress if I wasn't giving them the best experience every moment. There wasn't flexibility in how I parented and also in how I allowed them to be.

It took time to learn that my *connection* with my children was the most important piece in raising them. That also meant not looking at parenting as a job but looking at myself as a mom who was building close relationships with my children daily. My most important role was creating emotional safety for closeness. I realized the parent-child dyad has to be treated as a relationship for secure attachment to grow.

I discovered that my kids didn't need every experience to be free from disappointment or heartache. They needed me to comfort and reassure them in times of distress. I realized I didn't need to solve every problem that arose. It was about me listening, empathizing, and validating their experience. I gave up thinking that I would never hurt their feelings. It was about them being able to be transparent and share their discomfort, that I could repair their hurt. I recognized they didn't need to be productive and accomplish something every minute of the day. What was most important was experiencing joy in being together, when they felt my love the most. I let go of the notion that they would never be sad or mad or struggle. I realized how important it was for my presence to bring them comfort. They could reach out to me in times of need, and I was a person who brought reassurance that all would be okay.

I want to make sure you understand you don't have to be a perfect parent. There is really no such thing. My kids know I am imperfect, and that's okay. It allows them to be imperfect as well. Accepting our imperfections doesn't mean we don't continue to evolve. It means we can be honest in our relationships, and that brings closeness.

Conclusion: It's Never Too Late to Practice the Language of Connectedness with Your Teen(s)

At the heart of cultivating connectedness with your teen is self-reflection. Self-reflecting through the lens of a secure attachment matters within any relationship, but especially with our children. Being willing to ask yourself the needed questions to ensure how you are with your teen fosters feelings of connectedness.

With a secure attachment as the goal, building trust is foundational. Trust flourishes when you continually cultivate a sense of belonging at home by spending time in the mom or dad role—creating moments of joy and connection. Positive times of connection provide memories your teen can reflect on during times of stress to better cope.

You've learned so much in this book. You know that you can build trust in the many ways you communicate with your teen. Communicating with empathy and validation helps your teen feel your care and love. So focus on interaction with the goal of understanding your teen. When you look at every interaction as a learning experience, it can shift how you listen. You'll learn about your teen and about yourself simultaneously.

As you become more conscious of everything happening "within" you and "between" you and your teen when you communicate, be willing to look at ways disconnection is occurring. Look for the barriers that erode trust. Don't be afraid to look back at your family of origin and how that may be impacting how you are with your teen. Recognize that your past patterns may be embedded in your behavior today. Be aware that you may default to old patterns in times of stress. Mistakes will happen. Yet by making small efforts to evolve and change, you will in turn facilitate your relationship to evolve with your teen's changing needs. You can parent your teen as you wish you had been parented. Make changes that you know will bring security to your teen, which can bring pride and accomplishment to you. As you consciously shift the cycle of interaction with your teen and choose to volley, you will begin to see many changes.

The volley gives you structure to help support your interactions with your teen. The breakdown of the volley in chapter 6 provides a road map for you both to follow. Serving and returning back and forth (whether you disagree or not) becomes a co-regulating force as you share feelings and actively listen when your teen is in distress. The volley can also help you during times of conflict to de-escalate, slow things down, and listen to understand each other. The process of volleying enables you to stay connected.

Our experience is our reality. We bring that reality into our everyday interactions with others, and that includes our children. We only know what we know. Unless we self-reflect on our own upbringing and gain an understanding of how that impacts us and how we parent, the cycle may continue. It can feel like hard work to change what has been ingrained in us. It can feel like an undoing of the past. But it is never too late.

No matter our age, a feeling of connectedness with our primary attachment figure has a significant bearing on how we feel about ourselves. The relationship between parent and teen largely determines what a teen will expect from another in future relationships and is predictive of how their relationships will play out. You are your child's first love. You provide the lessons of what love looks and feels like.

Now it's time to ask your teen, "What is your experience in your relationship with me?" Be willing to listen and hear their answer. From one open heart to another, allow the transparency connectedness loop to flourish.

Self-Care and Coping

Self-Care

Life is busy for most parents. Work responsibilities, domestic duties, and caring for others sometimes mean you put yourself last on the priority list. To parent at your best, you need to take time for yourself. Balance your time connecting with others and spending moments in solitude. You need both. Prioritizing self-care each and every day improves your physical and mental health and helps you cope better in moments of stress. Everyone's needs are different; give yourself permission to find a formula for balance.

How to Fit in Self-Care

Try a Fifteen-Minute Vacation

- Sit quietly in the morning before anyone wakes up.
- Enjoy your coffee or tea while looking out the window.
- Meditate.
- Call a friend.
- Put the to-do list aside and take a walk in the middle of the workday.
- Let the water run a bit longer in the shower.
- Close your eyes and escape to your favorite place.
- Sit outside in the sun.
- Smile and say hi to someone else.
- Make music, play an instrument, or make a playlist.
- Light a candle or use pleasant aromas and close your eyes.
- Cuddle on the couch with someone you love.
- Listen to your favorite musical artist.

- Take a warm bath.
- Grab your earbuds or headphones and listen to bilateral music.
- Solicit a hug.
- Dance.
- Take a steam or sauna.
- Paint your nails your favorite color or do a home facial.
- Create, draw, color, knit.
- Play solitaire or do a crossword puzzle or sudoku.
- Listen to a comedy podcast.
- Take a drive, blast the music, and sing.

Make More Time to Fill Your Bucket

- Meet a friend or at least schedule a phone call or FaceTime to connect (ideally weekly).
- Move your body (daily): walk, run, bike, hike, play sports, do yoga.
- Read a book for pleasure.
- Sit by a body of water: find a lake, pond, or stream, and watch the ripples.
- Take a break from social media for a week.
- Join a sports league with a friend.
- Take up an instrument or singing lessons.
- Go fishing.
- Get a pedicure, manicure, or massage.
- Go "no screen" for the weekend.
- Visit the beach, watch the waves crash, and smell the sea air.
- Shoot baskets, hit tennis balls against a wall, or go to the golf driving range.
- Walk in nature.
- Discover a new hobby or reestablish an old one.
- Take a break from the news for a week.
- Garden.
- Cook a new recipe or bake.

- Go to the park, lie in the grass, look at the sky, and listen to the birds.
- Swim in a pool or natural body of water.
- Go to bed early.

Coping in the Moment

Decrease stress in the moment by acknowledging the stress as it arises. You can both self-regulate and reach out to another who can help calm you.

In the Moment

- Practice the breathing exercise from chapter 5.
- Try the five-senses grounding technique: name five things you see, four things you can touch, three things you hear, two things you can smell, and one thing you taste.
- Ask a trusted person for a hug or hand squeeze.
- Move your body: do push-ups or jumping jacks, take a walk, or get a change in scenery.
- Cuddle with your animal on the couch.
- Take a cold shower or a warm bath to help change your mood.
- Strike a yoga pose: downward dog, child's pose, or even a headstand.
- Use the negative self-talk process from chapter 5.
- Say out loud what you are saying to yourself in your head.
- Imagine turning to your friend or the younger you and telling them what you are saying to yourself.
- Focus on the present; ruminating tends to be about the past or future.
- Ask yourself, Is this helpful, kind, or necessary to tell myself?
- Think of a good memory or favorite person.
- Shift your thinking and make a mental gratitude list.
- Ask a friend or family member to just listen.
- Count backward from one hundred.

- Dump your thoughts and feelings on paper.
- Think of the difficulty in the moment passing like the weather changes.

Remember, "Perfection" Is Impossible

Keep in mind this slightly updated definition of perfection: "For humans, an impossibility, an unachievable state. An illusion some feel others have achieved. Trying to achieve it or holding a belief that it is possible will cause discomfort and likely create another issue or multiple issues."

Holding yourself to a high standard is good. But too often we require perfection from ourselves in our parenting, in our jobs, and while doing life. When it comes to being a parent, it is more important to simply connect with your kids and be there for them during both the good and the messy parts of life.

Resources

We can all use support at different times in our lives. All of us! Below is a list of resources from crisis to education and counseling options.[1]

Twenty-Four-Hour Crisis Support

988 Suicide & Crisis Lifeline (English and Spanish)
Call 988.
https://988lifeline.org/

Crisis Text Line (English and Spanish)
Text HOME to 741741.
https://www.crisistextline.org/

SAMHSA (Substance Abuse and Mental Health Services Administration) (English and Spanish)
Call 1-800-662-HELP (4357).
https://www.samhsa.gov/find-help/national-helpline

Veterans Crisis Line (English and Spanish)
Dial 988 and then press 1 or text 838255.
https://www.veteranscrisisline.net/get-help-now/chat/

The Trevor Project
Suicide prevention for LGBTQ+ young people
1-866-488-7386
https://www.thetrevorproject.org/get-help/

RAINN (English and Spanish)

Sexual assault hotline

1-800-656-HOPE (4673)

https://www.rainn.org/

Trans Lifeline (English and Spanish)

1-877 565-8860

https://translifeline.org/

Education and Support

NAMI (National Alliance on Mental Health)

https://www.nami.org/home

SAMHSA (Substance Abuse and Mental Health Services Administration)

https://www.samhsa.gov/

National Asian American Pacific Islander Mental Health Association

https://www.naapimha.org/

Active Minds

https://www.activeminds.org/

Anxiety & Depression Association of America

https://adaa.org/

National Eating Disorders Association

https://www.nationaleatingdisorders.org/

The Jed Foundation

https://jedfoundation.org/

Headspace

https://www.headspace.com/teens

Child Mind Institute

https://childmind.org/

The Liv Project

https://thelivproject.org/possible-side-effects-of-social-media/

Wait until 8th

https://www.waituntil8th.org

Counseling Services

SAMHSA (Substance Abuse and Mental Health Services Administration)

https://findtreatment.gov/

Health Center Program

Nationwide health center locator

https://findahealthcenter.hrsa.gov/

Teen Line

https://www.teenline.org/

Open Path Psychotherapy Collective

Nationwide/reduced rate

https://openpathcollective.org/

BEAM (Black Emotional and Mental Health)

https://wellness.beam.community/

Clinicians of Color
https://www.cliniciansofcolor.org/

Latinx Therapy
https://latinxtherapy.com/

Therapy for Black Girls
https://therapyforblackgirls.com/

Therapy for Black Men
https://therapyforblackmen.org/

Asian Mental Health Collective
https://www.asianmhc.org/therapists/

South Asian Mental Health Initiative & Network
https://samhin.org/

Inclusive Therapists
https://www.inclusivetherapists.com/

Free Black Therapy
https://www.freeblacktherapy.org/

Melanin & Mental Health
https://www.melaninandmentalhealth.com/

National Queer & Trans Therapist of Color Network
https://nqttcn.com/en/

Suicide Prevention

Suicide Stop International Help Center

https://www.suicidestop.com/

International Association for Suicide Prevention

https://www.iasp.info/

Suicide Prevention Resource Center

https://sprc.org/

American Foundation for Suicide Prevention

https://afsp.org/

The Trevor Project

https://www.thetrevorproject.org/

Now Matters Now

https://nowmattersnow.org/

The Liv Project

https://thelivproject.org/

Discussion Guides (English and Spanish)

https://thelivproject.org/worried-about-myself/

https://thelivproject.org/worried-about-someone/

Acknowledgments

This book would not be possible without my connections with others. My clients over the last twenty years granted me their trust by sharing their innermost thoughts and feelings. Thank you to the many who I have had the privilege of listening to. Each and every teen, parent, couple, and family gave me therapeutic insights and ultimately inspired me to put words to paper.

Heather Bowen Ray met with me once a week for six consecutive months while I wrote my first draft. Heather kept me on task and focused and helped me become a better writer. Her encouragement and feedback as a mother herself was invaluable. Thank you, Heather.

Sorina Rosoiu, my graphic designer, took my hand sketches and turned them into something beautiful. Thank you, Sorina. You are brilliant at what you do.

Mark Fretz and Evan Phail from Radius Book Group took a chance on me and walked me through the publishing process. Danny Constantino ensured the book was polished while putting up with my grammatical errors that I should have learned in seventh grade. Much gratitude for you all at Radius.

I will always be indebted to my mentors over the years: Megan Cook, Grant Tschetter, and my most recent, Patti Swope (to name a few). There is always more to learn about the human condition.

Many mental health professionals and parents read this book and provided an endorsement. Thank you for your time and kind words. I will forever be grateful.

Special thanks to author Curt Pessmen, who read my first chapter, served as a mentor, and encouraged me to keep writing.

Thank you to all my family and friends (including Mom and Dad) who read chapters, provided feedback, and returned all my texts of sample titles and covers. I know it was a lot!

Jamie, my husband, best friend, and partner in raising our children—you are an inspiration and a model for hard work and dedication to caring for others and family. You encouraged me in my many moments of doubt while writing this book.

To my three children, Emma, Jack, and Olivia (two of whom are now adults), you are my biggest teachers. Over the years, I continually had to look inside myself to understand my own tendencies and their origin and discover how to move differently during our interactions.

My family, I cherish my time with each of you individually and us together as a whole. Being around you four gives me such an internal warmth and endless joy in my life. I would never choose to do life with anyone else. You are my favorite people. And if the book is a flop, I know you all still love me—that's all that matters.

Notes

Chapter 1: Connectedness

1 R. W. Blum, J. Lai, M. Martinez, and C. Jessee, "Adolescent Connectedness: Cornerstone for Health and Wellbeing," *BMJ* 379 (2022): e069213, https://doi.org/10.1136/bmj-2021-069213.

2 C. E. Foster, A. Horwitz, A. Thomas, K. Opperman, P. Gipson, A. Burnside, D. M. Stone, and C. A. King, "Connectedness to Family, School, Peers, and Community in Socially Vulnerable Adolescents," *Children and Youth Services Review* 81 (2017): 321–31, https://www.ncbi.nlm.nih.gov/pmc/articles/PMC6128354/.

3 Vivek H. Murthy, "Our Epidemic of Loneliness and Isolation," US Department of Health and Human Services, May 3, 2023, https://www.hhs.gov/sites/default/files/surgeon-general-social-connection-advisory.pdf; Vivek H. Murthy, "Protecting Youth Mental Health," US Department of Health and Human Services, December 6, 2021, https://www.hhs.gov/sites/default/files/surgeon-general-youth-mental-health-advisory.pdf.

4 "Parent-Child Bond Predicts Depression, Anxiety in Teens Attending High-Achieving Schools," ScienceDaily, October 25, 2018, https://www.sciencedaily.com/releases/2018/10/181025141007.htm.

5 Susan M. Johnson, *Attachment Theory in Practice: Emotionally Focused Therapy (EFT) with Individuals, Couples, and Families* (New York: Guilford Press, 2019), 76.

6 K. Dubois-Comtois, C. Cyr, K. Pascuzzo, and M. Lessard, "Attachment Theory in Clinical Work with Adolescents," *Journal of Child and Adolescent Behavior* 1 (2013): 111, https://www.omicsonline.org/open-access/attachment-theory-in-clinical-work-with-adolescents-2375-4494.1000111.php?aid=20894.

7 Philip A. Fisher, "Parenting for Brain Development and Prosperity," Center on the Developing Child at Harvard University, November 15, 2017, https://developingchild.harvard.edu/resources/parenting-for-brain-development-and-prosperity/.

8 M. M. Moretti and M. Peled, "Adolescent-Parent Attachment: Bonds That Support Healthy Development," *Paediatrics & Child Health* 9, no. 8 (2004): 551–55, https://doi.org/10.1093/pch/9.8.551.

Chapter 2: Belonging

1 Saga Pardede and Velibor Bobo Kovač, "Distinguishing the Need to Belong
   and Sense of Belongingness: The Relation between Need to Belong and
   Personal Appraisals under Two Different Belongingness—Conditions,"
   European Journal of Investigation in Health, Psychology and Education 13, no. 2
   (2023): 331–44, https://www.ncbi.nlm.nih.gov/pmc/articles/PMC9955914/#:
   ~:text=People%20have%20a%20fundamental%20need,3%2C4%2C5%5D.

2 Zoë Rejaän, Inge E. van der Valk, and Susan Branje, "The Role of Sense of
   Belonging and Family Structure in Adolescent Adjustment," *Journal of Research
   on Adolescence* 32, no. 4 (2022): 1354–68, https://www.ncbi.nlm.nih.gov/pmc/
   articles/PMC10078782/.

3 Valarie King and Lisa M. Boyd, "Factors Associated with Perceptions of
   Family Belonging among Adolescents," *Journal of Marriage and Family* 78, no. 4
   (2016): 1114–30, https://www.ncbi.nlm.nih.gov/pmc/articles/PMC5054750/.

4 James House, Karl Landis, and Debra Umberson, "Social Relationships and
   Health," *Science* 241 (1988): 540–45, https://doi.org/10.1126/science.3399889.

5 Susan Caso, "Comforting Part 5: Comforting Your Teen Series Conclusion,"
   Susan Caso, MA, LPC, March 4, 2023, https://susancaso.com/comforting-you
   -teen-series-part-five/.

6 Susan Caso, "Under Pressure: Are We Asking Too Much from Our Teens?,"
   Liv Project, January 10, 2023, https://thelivproject.org/under-pressure-are-we
   -asking-too-much-from-our-teens/.

7 C. Ryan, D. Huebner, R. M. Diaz, and J. Sanchez, "Family Rejection as a
   Predictor of Negative Health Outcomes in White and Latino Lesbian, Gay, and
   Bisexual Young Adults," *American Academy of Pediatrics* 123, no. 1 (2009): 346–
   52, https://doi.org/10.1542/peds.2007-3524.

8 Kiley Hurst, "More Than Half of Americans Live within an Hour of Extended
   Family," Pew Research Center, May 18, 2022, https://www.pewresearch.org/
   short-reads/2022/05/18/more-than-half-of-americans-live-within-an-hour-of
   -extended-family/.

9 Samantha Krauss, Ulrich Orth, and Richard W. Robins, "Family Environment
   and Self-Esteem Development: A Longitudinal Study from Age 10 to 16,"
   Journal of Personality and Social Psychology, August 2020, https://www.ncbi
   .nlm.nih.gov/pmc/articles/PMC7080605/; "Research on the Importance of
   Multigenerational, Extended, and Forged Family Bonds: Foundation for
   Family Life," Foundation for Family Life, December 15, 2022, https://fflut.org/

general-topics/research-on-the-importance-of-multigenerational-extended
-and-forged-family-bonds/.

10 Roy F. Baumeister and Mark R. Leary, "The Need to Belong: Desire for
Interpersonal Attachments as a Fundamental Human Motivation," *Psychological
Bulletin* 117, no. 3 (1995): 497–529, https://doi.org/10.1037/0033-2909.117.3.497.

11 APA Dictionary of Psychology, American Psychological Association, s.v.
"bullying," accessed March 19, 2024, https://dictionary.apa.org/bullying.

12 Ming-Te Wang and Sarah Kenny, "Longitudinal Links between Father's and
Mothers' Harsh Verbal Discipline and Adolescents' Conduct Problems and
Depressive Symptoms," *Child Development* 85, no. 3 (2014): 908–23, https://
www.ncbi.nlm.nih.gov/pmc/articles/PMC3875601/.

13 APA Dictionary of Psychology, American Psychological Association,
s.v. "emotional abuse," last modified April 19, 2018, https://dictionary.apa
.org/emotional-abuse.

14 Wang and Kenny, "Longitudinal Links."

15 Frederick Rivara, "Preventing Bullying through Science, Policy, and Practice,"
National Library of Medicine, September 14, 2016, https://www.ncbi.nlm.nih
.gov/books/NBK390414/.

16 "Fast Facts: Preventing Adverse Childhood Experiences," Centers for Disease
Control and Prevention, June 29, 2023, https://www.cdc.gov/aces/about/?CDC
_AAref_Val=https://www.cdc.gov/violenceprevention/aces/fastfact.html.

17 "Fast Facts."

18 "Fast Facts."

Chapter 3: Effective Communication

1 Laura M. Dimler, Misaki N. Natsuaki, Paul D. Hastings, Carolyn Zahn-
Waxler, and Bonnie Klimes-Dougan, "Parenting Effects Are in the Eye of the
Beholder: Parent-Adolescent Differences in Perceptions Affects Adolescent
Problem Behaviors," *Journal of Youth and Adolescence* 46, no. 5 (2016): 1076–88,
https://doi.org/10.1007/s10964-016-0612-1; Juli Fraga, "Parents Don't Get
How Negative They Seem to Their Teenagers," *Time*, December 16, 2016,
https://time.com/4604907/parents-dont-get-how-negative-they-seem-to
-their-teenagers/.

2 Lauren Sharkey, "What Does It Mean to Be Touch Starved?," Healthline,
April 8, 2021, https://www.healthline.com/health/touch-starved#benefits-of
-touch.

3 Alexandra Benisek, "Touch Starvation: What to Know," WebMD, September 15, 2023, https://www.webmd.com/balance/touch-starvation.

4 Melissa Milsten, "Yale Study: Parents Demonstrating Warmth Reduce Conflict with Teens," Grown and Flown, August 2020, https://grownandflown.com/parent-teen-conflict-reduced-with-warmth-love-yale-study/; Ying Chen, Laura D. Kubzansky, and Tyler J. VanderWeele, "Parental Warmth and Flourishing in Mid-life," *Social Science & Medicine* 220 (2019): 65–72, https://doi.org/10.1016/j.socscimed.2018.10.026.

Chapter 4: Self-Reflection on Your Past

1 Peter C. Costello, *Attachment-Based Psychotherapy: Helping Patients Develop Adaptive Capacities* (Washington, DC: American Psychological Association, 2015).

2 Dubois-Comtois et al., "Attachment Theory in Clinical Work."

3 Terrence Sanvictores and Magda D. Mendez, "Types of Parenting Styles and Effects on Children," National Library of Medicine, September 18, 2022, https://www.ncbi.nlm.nih.gov/books/NBK568743/.

4 Leigh Karavasillis, Anna Beth Doyle, and Dorothy Markiewicz, "Associations between Parenting Style and Attachment to Mother in Middle Childhood and Adolescence," *International Journal of Behavioral Development* 27, no. 2 (2003): 153–64, https://www.researchgate.net/publication/247778904_Associations_between_Parenting_Style_and_Attachment_to_Mother_in_Middle_Childhood_and_Adolescence.

5 Ali Zeinali, Hassanpasha Sharifi, Mirsalahadine Enayati, Parviz Asgari, and Gohlamreza Pasha, "The Mediational Pathway among Parenting Styles, Attachment Styles and Self-Regulation with Addiction Susceptibility of Adolescents," *Journal of Research in Medical Sciences* 16, no. 9 (2011): 1105–21, https://www.ncbi.nlm.nih.gov/pmc/articles/PMC3430035/.

6 I. O. Henriksen, I. Ranøyen, M. S. Indredavik, and F. Stenseng, "The Role of Self-Esteem in the Development of Psychiatric Problems: A Three-Year Prospective Study in a Clinical Sample of Adolescents," *Child and Adolescent Psychiatry and Mental Health* 11 (2017): 68, https://www.ncbi.nlm.nih.gov/pmc/articles/PMC5747942/.

7 APA Dictionary of Psychology, American Psychological Association, s.v. "trauma," accessed March 19, 2024, https://dictionary.apa.org/trauma.

8 "Fast Facts."

9 Rachel Yehuda and Amy Lehrner, "Intergenerational Transmission of Trauma Effects: Putative Role of Epigenetic Mechanisms," *World Psychiatry* 17, no. 3 (2018): 243–57, https://www.ncbi.nlm.nih.gov/pmc/articles/PMC6127768/.

10 Bruce D. Perry and Oprah Winfrey, *What Happened to You? Conversations on Trauma, Resilience, and Healing* (New York: Flatiron, 2021), 61.

11 Marc H. Bornstein, "Culture, Parenting, and Zero-to-Threes," *Zero to Three*, March 2015, https://www.ncbi.nlm.nih.gov/pmc/articles/PMC5865595/.

12 Jeronimo Cortina and Shana Hardin, "The Geography of Mental Health, Urbanicity, and Affluence," *International Journal of Environmental Research and Public Health*, April 7, 2023, https://www.ncbi.nlm.nih.gov/pmc/articles/PMC10138034/.

13 "Generational Differences Chart," West Midland Family Centers, accessed April 12, 2024, http://www.wmfc.org/uploads/generationaldifferenceschart.pdf.

14 Jonathan Rothwell, "Teens Spend Average of 4.8 Hours on Social Media per Day," Gallup, October 13, 2023, https://news.gallup.com/poll/512576/teens-spend-average-hours-social-media-per-day.aspx.

15 Sophie Bethune, "Gen Z More Likely to Report Mental Health Concerns," *Monitor on Psychology*, January 2019, https://www.apa.org/monitor/2019/01/gen-z.

Chapter 5: Introspection

1 Perry and Winfrey, *What Happened to You?*

2 Fran Simone, "Negative Self-Talk: Don't Let It Overwhelm You," *Psychology Today*, December 4, 2017, https://www.psychologytoday.com/us/blog/family-affair/201712/negative-self-talk-dont-let-it-overwhelm-you.

Chapter 6: Between

1 "A Guide on How to Treat a Rebellious Teen," Newport Academy, October 25, 2023, https://www.newportacademy.com/resources/restoring-families/rebellious-teen/#:~:text=By%20rebelling%20against%20authority%2C%20teenagers,individuation%20of%20the%20adolescent%20personality.

2 R. C. Kessler, G. P. Amminger, S. Aguilar-Gaxiola, J. Alonso, S. Lee, and T. B. Ustün, "Age of Onset of Mental Disorders: A Review of Recent Literature,"

Current Opinion in Psychiatry 20, no. 4 (2007): 359–64, https://pubmed.ncbi.nlm
.nih.gov/17551351/.

3 Kristin Moore, Elizabeth C. Hair, and Laura Lippman, "Parent-Teen
Relationships and Interactions: Far More Positive Than Not," Research Gate,
January 2004, https://www.researchgate.net/publication/265145581_Parent
-Teen_Relationships_and_Interactions_Far_More_Positive_Than_Not.

Chapter 7: External Influences That Cause Stress and Disconnection

1 Johann Hari, *Stolen Focus: Why You Can't Pay Attention* (London: Bloomsbury
Publishing, 2023).

2 Daniel J. Levitin, "Why the Modern World Is Bad for Your Brain," *Guardian*,
January 18, 2015, https://www.theguardian.com/science/2015/jan/18/modern
-world-bad-for-brain-daniel-j-levitin-organized-mind-information-overload.

3 Brooke Auxier, "Parenting Children in the Age of Screens," Pew Research
Center, July 28, 2020, https://www.pewresearch.org/internet/2020/07/28/
parenting-children-in-the-age-of-screens/.

4 Lisa Brussell, MEd, personal communication with author, April 1, 2024.

5 Daniel J. Siegel, *Brainstorm: The Power and Purpose of the Teenage Brain*
(Vancouver, BC: Langara College, 2017); "Teen Brain: Behavior, Problem
Solving, and Decision Making," American Academy of Child and Adolescent
Psychiatry, September 2017, https://www.aacap.org/AACAP/Families_and
_Youth/Facts_for_Families/FFF-Guide/The-Teen-Brain-Behavior-Problem
-Solving-and-Decision-Making-095.aspx; "Stressed Out: Teens and Adults
Respond Differently," National Science Foundation, September 3, 2010,
https://new.nsf.gov/news/stressed-out-teens-adults-respond-differently.

6 "Estimated Probability of Competing in College Athletics," NCAA, accessed
March 20, 2024, https://www.ncaa.org/sports/2015/3/2/estimated-probability
-of-competing-in-college-athletics.aspx.

7 Kirsten Weir, "Social Media Brings Benefits and Risks to Teens: Psychology
Can Help Identify a Path Forward," *Monitor on Psychology*, September 1, 2023,
https://www.apa.org/monitor/2023/09/protecting-teens-on-social-media.

8 Emily A. Vogels, "Teens and Cyberbullying 2022," Pew Research Center,
December 15, 2022, https://www.pewresearch.org/internet/2022/12/15/teens
-and-cyberbullying-2022/.

9 Eva S. Lefkowitz, Sara A. Vasilenko, Rose Wesche, and Jennifer L. Maggs, "Changes in Diverse Sexual and Contraceptive Behaviors across College," *Journal of Sex Research*, October 2019, https://www.ncbi.nlm.nih.gov/pmc/articles/PMC6411451/.

10 Wen-Hsu Lin, Chia-Hua Liu, and Chin-Chun Yi, "Exposure to Sexually Explicit Media in Early Adolescence Is Related to Risky Sexual Behavior in Emerging Adulthood," *PLoS One* 15, no. 4 (2020): e0230242, https://www.ncbi.nlm.nih.gov/pmc/articles/PMC7147756/.

11 "Talking with Your Teens about Sex," Centers for Disease Control and Prevention, November 21, 2019, https://www.cdc.gov/healthyyouth/protective/factsheets/talking_teens.htm.

12 Jenny S. Radesky, "Mobile Device Use for Calming and Emotional Reactivity and Executive Functioning in Young Children," *JAMA Pediatrics*, January 1, 2023, https://jamanetwork.com/journals/jamapediatrics/article-abstract/2799042; Caroline Fitzpatrick, Elizabeth Harvey, Emma Cristini, Angélique Laurent, Jean-Pascal Lemelin, and Gabrielle Garon-Carrier, "Is the Association between Early Childhood Screen Media Use and Effortful Control Bidirectional? A Prospective Study during the COVID-19 Pandemic," *Frontiers in Psychology*, June 27, 2022, https://www.ncbi.nlm.nih.gov/pmc/articles/PMC9271860/.

13 Ron Taffel and Melinda Blau, *The Second Family: How Adolescent Power Is Challenging the American Family* (New York: St. Martin's Press, 2001).

14 Murthy, "Our Epidemic of Loneliness and Isolation."

Chapter 8: Modeling Healthy Adult Relationships

1 Patrick T. Davis and E. Mark Cummings, "Marital Conflict and Child Adjustment: An Emotional Security Hypothesis," Research Gate, 1994, https://www.researchgate.net/publication/15390513_Marital_Conflict_and_Child_Adjustment_An_Emotional_Security_Hypothesis.

2 Chanell Washington and Lydia Anderson, "Is Your State in Step with National Marriage and Divorce Trends?," US Census, July 11, 2023, https://www.census.gov/library/stories/2023/07/marriage-divorce-rates.html#:~:text=Both%20the%20marriage%20and%20divorce,per%201%2C000%20women%20in%202011.

3 Wendy Wang, "The U.S. Divorce Rate Has Hit a 50-Year Low," Institute for Family Studies, November 10, 2020, https://ifstudies.org/blog/the-us-divorce-rate-has-hit-a-50-year-low.

4 Ann Buscho, "Understanding the Effects of High-Conflict Divorce on Kids," *Psychology Today*, December 18, 2019, https://www.psychologytoday.com/us/blog/better-divorce/201912/understanding-the-effects-high-conflict-divorce-kids.

5 APA Dictionary of Psychology, American Psychological Association, s.v. "parental alienation syndrome (PAS)," accessed March 19, 2024, https://dictionary.apa.org/parental-alienation-syndrome.

Chapter 9: Transparency and Connectedness, a Positive Feedback Loop

1 Cited in Beth Clark and Nina Preto, "Exploring the Concept of Vulnerability in Health Care," *Canadian Medical Association Journal* 190, no. 11 (2018): E308–9, https://www.ncbi.nlm.nih.gov/pmc/articles/PMC5860890/#:~:text=The%20Oxford%20English%20Dictionary%20defines,this%20concept%20in%20health%20care.

2 Brene Brown, *Daring Greatly: How the Courage to Be Vulnerable Transforms the Way We Live, Love, Parent, and Lead* (New York: Penguin Random House, 2017), 2.

3 Murthy, "Protecting Youth Mental Health."

4 Sally C. Curtin, "National Vital Statistics Reports," Centers for Disease Control and Prevention, September 11, 2020, https://www.cdc.gov/nchs/data/nvsr/nvsr69/nvsr-69-11-508.pdf.

5 "Youth Risk Behavior Survey Data Summary & Trends Report," Centers for Disease Control and Prevention, February 13, 2023, https://www.cdc.gov/healthyyouth/data/yrbs/pdf/yrbs_data-summary-trends_report2023_508.pdf.

6 "Suicide Rising across the US," Centers for Disease Control and Prevention, June 2018, https://www.cdc.gov/vitalsigns/pdf/vs-0618-suicide-H.pdf.

7 "Mental Health of Adolescents," World Health Organization, November 17, 2021, https://www.who.int/news-room/fact-sheets/detail/adolescent-mental-health.

8 Flavia Izzo, Roberto Baiocco, and Jessica Pistella, "Children's and Adolescents' Happiness and Family Functioning: A Systematic Literature Review," *International Journal of Environmental Research and Public Health*, December 10, 2022, https://www.ncbi.nlm.nih.gov/pmc/articles/PMC9778774/.

9 Corinne Rees, "Childhood Attachment," *British Journal of General Practice*, November 2007, https://www.ncbi.nlm.nih.gov/pmc/articles/PMC2169321/.

Resources

1 These resources are provided for informational purposes only. Their inclusion does not guarantee the quality of services rendered. Users are encouraged to exercise discretion and independently verify the suitability and reliability of each before engaging in its services. The author and publisher are not responsible for any outcomes resulting from the use of these resources.